P9-EDR-218

The Junior League of Hampton Roads, Inc. Presented by

Children's
PARTY BOOK

Junior League of Hampton Roads, Inc.

729 Thimble Shoals Boulevard, Suite 4D

Newport News, Virginia 23606

Copyright 1984
The Junior League of Hampton Roads, Inc.

First Printing , December 1984, 5,000 Copies
Second Printing, January 1986, 5,000 Copies
Third Printing, November 1987, 5,000 Copies
Fourth Printing, January 1989, 5,000 Copies
Fifth Printing, November 1990, 5,000 Copies
Sixth Printing (revised and updated), April 1996, 10,000 Copies
Seventh Printing, September 1998, 10,000 Copies

Acknowledgements

Graphic Design & Illustration.......... Gnomads Graphics
Editing.......... Sharon Goldsworthy

Manufactured by
Favorite Recipes® Press
an imprint of

FRP™

P.O. Box 305142
Nashville, Tennessee 37230
800-358-0560

ISBN 0-9613600-3-8
LCCN 96-75026

PARTY BOOK COMMITTEE

CHAIRMAN
Rebecca Fass

COMMITTEE MEMBERS

Jennifer Barr	Laura Lynn Luce
Sidney Jordan	Cathy Maples
Nan Kane	Elizabeth Mayo
Allison LeCuyer	Jane Shuart

Ann Spinelli

The Junior League of Hampton Roads, Inc. is an organization of women committed to promoting voluntarism and to improving the community through the effective action and leadership of trained volunteers. Its purpose is exclusively educational and charitable. Through its volunteer efforts in the areas of child welfare, women's health, family issues, literacy, and the arts and humanities, the Junior League of Hampton Roads, Inc. serves and enriches its community. Profits from the sale of **Children's Party Book** are returned to the community through the projects of the Junior League of Hampton Roads, Inc.

TABLE OF CONTENTS

INTRODUCTION

The original **Children's Party Book** was developed a decade ago as a means to support the community projects of the Junior League of Hampton Roads, Inc. At that time, the book was one of only a few books devoted to parties for children. Now there are more books available, and to stay current with the times, we have updated and revised our popular classic. The 25 fully developed parties in this book have even more ideas for decorations, favors, games and activities, as well as invitations that can be easily photocopied or created at home. Three new sections have been added. One contains 20 additional party themes that are briefly elaborated, another tells how to adapt many different games and activities, and the third has ideas for school parties. The recipe section at the end of the book contains the most popular recipes from the original book along with many new recipes that children are sure to love.

The parties in this book have been designed to appeal to a wide variety of children. When planning your child's party, be sure to include him or her as much as possible in the planning process. Use your imaginations together to create the perfect party that fits your family's style, accomodations and budget. Begin the planning process early by choosing the theme and reading the suggestions for that theme (feel free to use fun ideas from the other parties, too). Make your guest list and mentally walk through the entire party. Make a contingency plan for different problems that may arise. For instance, if you are planning an outdoor party, have either a rain date or alternate inside activities planned. If you do move your party indoors, have some plastic tablecloths ready to spread on the floor of the party room to protect the floor. Have plenty of food and favors for extra guests, such as siblings of invited guests, who may join the fun at the last minute.

If you have a computer or video games, put them off limits to keep children from playing with them instead of participating in the party. The shy party guest (or the child who misses his or her parents), can be brought into the party spirit by being made your helper. Make sure your invitation to him or her is warm, friendly and also direct, such as "Let's serve the food". Asking if the child would like to help will probably result in a negative answer.

To prepare for parents who are late picking up their children, have an activity planned "just in case". A video of short cartoons works well. To avoid this problem altogether, offer in advance to drive your guests home, or organize a carpool.

Begin your party preparations as soon as possible. Many decorations, foods and crafts can be made well in advance of the big day. Try to leave as little as possible for the party day. It also helps to have a flexible activity for your arriving guests to do, so that they will not immediately go to your child's room and play. Try serving party foods in sequence, to keep the children in their chairs longer. Have another activity planned for the fast eaters while the slower ones finish their food. Last of all, try to relax and remember that this is your child's day. It's the perfect opportunity for you to pay special attention to him or her all day and to show your love.

Jennifer Johnson, Age 8

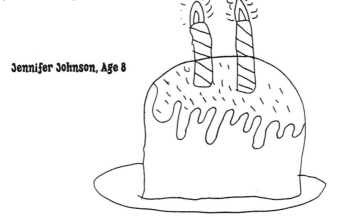

The children's illustrations found throughout this book were drawn by local children. They reflect the natural imagination and creativity that all children have. Our thanks go to the parents for allowing us to benefit from their children's talents and to the children for creating such fun artwork.

You are invited to a

JURASSIC PARTY

Come to a monstrously fun party for

_____

that you'll really dig!

The address is

The party is on

from   to

If you can't make it,

please call

JURASSIC PARTY

Invitations:

Copy the designed invitation provided.

Decorations & Favors:

• Cut dinosaur paw prints out of green paper and make a trail from the sidewalk to the party house's door. Decorate with more footprints inside.

• Decorate a white paper tablecloth with dinosaur paw prints. Trace the paw print pattern on a potato half. Cut away the excess edges. Dip it in green paint and go to town!

• Use the **DINOSAUR CAKE** as the focal point of the table.

• Use "dinosaur egg" candy or large jaw breakers as favors. Give out candy corn and call it "dinosaur teeth".

MENU

Dinoburgers

Stegosaurus Salad

Pterodactyl Eggs

Lochness Bars

Dinosaur Cake

T.Rex Punch

Dinosaur Paw Print

Games & Activities:

• Play **FOLLOW THE LEADER** following the dinosaur trail.

• Have the children go for a **DIG**. Hide small prizes in the far side of the backyard or in a cooperative neighbor's yard. Tie a piece of yarn to each of the favors. Walk the yarn back to the birthday house, but take care to make the path interesting-around trees, over logs, etc. When it's time to **DIG**, each child must follow his or her string to discover a prize.

• Cover a tissue box with green construction paper, leaving the hole open. Tape toes to the front side of the box. Children can wear these **BIG FOOT SHOES** for a planned race or just for fun!

• Use the **PLAY CLAY** recipe to make your own monsters. The recipe and directions are in the recipe section of this book. Have this made ahead of time and tinted in good monster colors like green ,purple and red. Cover squares of cardboard with aluminum foil to make trays to take these creatures home.

• Play **TRICERATOPS RING TOSS**. Either paint a large board to resemble a triceratops and use dowels as the horns, or simply use a plain dowel and toss rings over the pretend horn.

• **PIN THE TAIL ON THE DINOSAUR** is always a hit, too.

• Play **DANCING DINOSAURS**. Children pretend to be dinosaurs dancing to music. Periodically stop the music and the little dinosaurs must freeze. Start the music again and the dancing resumes.

• Gather leaves, shells and rocks to imprint in clay to create your own **FOSSILS**. Make a round ball of clay and then flatten it. Press the object into the clay and remove, leaving an impression in the clay. Follow the directions that come with the clay for drying the fossils.

Chuck Ostendorff, Age 11

Courtney Cocke, Age 8

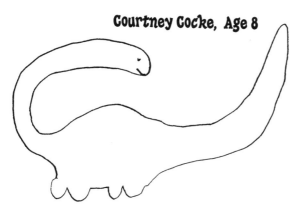

YOU ARE INVITED TO A NATURE PARTY!

WHEN _____

WHERE _____

GIVEN BY _____

BACK TO NATURE

Invitations:

Copy the designed invitation and let your child color it.

Nicholas Bryant, Age 3

Decorations & Favors:

• Hang a bird silhouette mobile over the party table.

• Decorate brown paper bags with leaf rubbings and then let the children use the bags to take home their party favors.

• Plastic bugs, bug rings, animal stickers, and Zoo discount coupons can be put into the goodie bags as favors.

• This party could easily be turned into a camp-out or a sleepover. Activities could include flashlight tag, catching fireflies, and roasting marshmallows on the campfire.

• Give flashlights with batteries and jars for bugs as favors for a campout.

Marshall Jordan, Age 3

MENU

Pigs in a Blanket

Carrot & Celery Sticks

Trail Mix

Chocolate Fondue
with Fruit

Dirt Cups
with Gummie Worms

Ladybug Cake

Rainbow Floats

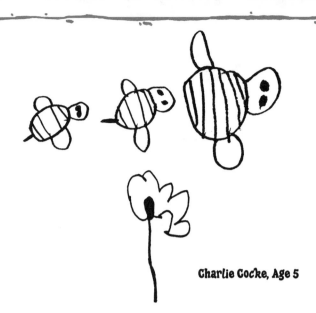

Charlie Cocke, Age 5

Games & Activities:

• Make **BIRD FEEDERS** out of large pine cones. Tie a string around the cone and make a loop for a hanger. Cover the ends of the cones with peanut butter and dip in birdseed.

• Also, for the feathered friends, string **FOOD CHAINS** to hang on the trees, made out of popcorn, dried fruit, raisins, and cranberries.

• Make **SUN PRINTS**. Look in museums or camera stores for a special type of paper that is sensitive to sunlight. Place leaves or flowers on the paper and let the sun do its magic!

• Decorate **FLOWER POTS** . Use small clay pots and let children decorate with paints or attach small pine cones, leaves, and acorns with white glue. Then plant small plants or herbs in the pots.

• **BUG EYES**. Cut egg cartons, separating egg cups into pairs, and punch holes through the centers to make two eyes. Attach pipe cleaners to secure them to the head like eyeglasses. Attach additional pipe cleaners for antennas and decorate accordingly.

• Try this variation of Musical Chairs, called **MUSICAL FROGS**. Cut green lily pads from poster board and tape to the floor in a circle. Play the song "Talk to the Animals", and have children jump like frogs from pad to pad. Proceed as with musical chairs by removing a lily pad after each round of music.

• Go on a **SCAVENGER HUNT**. Divide the children into two teams and give each team a list of nature items to find. As they find an item they can mark it off the list.

Here are some examples of things to find: seed pods, leaves, sticks, rocks, shells, feathers, flower petals, birds, animal homes, animal tracks, spider webs, and cocoons.

For older children, have a **RECYCLING SCAVENGER HUNT**. Go to pre-arranged homes of neighbors and friends with a list of recyclables such as aluminum cans, newspaper, film cannisters, styrofoam, paper bags, grocery bags, jar lids, and egg cartons. The team that returns with the most variety wins.

Bird Beak Straws

Cut bird beaks out of yellow or orange contact paper. Do not remove the backing. Add large round bird eyes. Thread drinking straws through two slits cut in the beaks and sip away!

Swing over to this
part of the jungle
for a
Wild Party!

For

When

Where

R.S.V.P.

WILD PARTY

Invitations:

Copy the designed invitation provided.

Decorations & Favors:

• Bring out all of the stuffed animals that your child owns.

• Create a fanciful animal menagerie from assorted marshmallows, cereals and gumdrops held together by pretzel sticks. These sweet creatures make cute table decorations and can follow the children home as favors.

• Cut simple leaf shapes from green construction paper, staple them to strips of green gift wrap yarn and hang these vines around the party room.

• Use blue, green or yellow streamers and lots of balloons to create the jungle mood.

• Fill small plastic buckets with jungle books, animal crackers, stickers, and/or coloring books.

• Creepy rubber reptiles and shell beads also make great favors.

MENU

Snake Sandwich

Monkey Bread or

Tropical Fruit Tray

Peanutty Monkey Bars

Lion Cake

Jungle Punch

Thumbprint Animals

Games & Activities:

• Play **JUNGLE JUMBLE** by having the children sit in a circle of chairs. Use one less chair than the number of children and have the extra child stand in the middle. Make a list of animal names to be used by the child in the middle, and assign one name each to two or three children in chairs.
The game begins with the child in the middle calling out an animal name from the list. The children with that name try to exchange seats without the child in the middle sitting in one of their seats. The child without a seat becomes the caller in the middle.

• Try **THUMBPRINT PICTURES**. Use an inkpad and make several fingerprints on a piece of paper; then add wings, ears, tails, and snouts to create a collection of animals.

• Play **NET THE ANIMAL.** For one net, four children hold hands to form a circle, and one child is the animal. The children chase the "animal" and must catch him inside the circle without dropping hands.

• To play **ELEPHANT WALK**, divide your group into equal teams. The first child extends one arm out in front for his trunk and one arm between his legs for his tail. The second child holds the first child's tail and extends his arm through his legs for the third child to hold onto. Continue the line until each child is holding an elephant's tail in front of him. Have the teams race, and the first one to reach the finish line without dropping hands, wins.

• Play **MONKEY TAG**. Scatter the group as for tag. Pick one or more children to be "It". "It" must hold up one hand in the air all the time he is chasing the others. The only way a runner may be safe from being tagged is to touch a tree. Allow no player to spend too much time on the safety zone in order to keep the game active.

• Play **ZOODLES**. Divide players into two teams and provide each with paper and pencil. One child from each team is told the name of an animal. He or she must then communicate this identity to the team by drawing the animal. Make sure that everyone has the chance to be an artist.

• Try a **PUSH-ME-PULL-YOU** race. Have the children interlock their arms with partners, while standing back-to-back. Race from starting to finish line, one child walking forward, one walking backward.

• For the younger set, try **TALK TO THE ANIMALS**, a "Simon Says" type game. Call things out like, "Birds fly" or "Bunnies hop", and the children do the motions accordingly. But they'll eliminate themselves by flapping their wings when you call out "Elephants fly" or meowing when you call out "Dogs meow" or any other inappropriate command.

Tommy Feild, Age 9

Turner Donaldson, Age 5

Madeline LeCuyer, Age 7

Your favorite bear is invited to a Tag Along Teddy Bear Party!

Please tag along for a fun time!

When

Where

Given by

TAG ALONG TEDDY

Invitations:

Copy the designed invitation provided. It indicates that each teddy bear is to have a child "tag along" and join in the fun.

Decorations & Favors:

• Bears that attend the party will provide much of the decoration.

• Print a paper tablecloth with a bear-shaped cookie cutter dipped in paint. Use the **TEDDY BEAR CAKE** as a centerpiece.

• Decorate small baskets for each child and fill with small bear shaped cookies and candy.

MENU

Peanut Butter & Honey
Sandwiches

Honey Bee Ambrosia

Big Bear Sundaes

Teddy Bear Cake

Apple Juice

Menu Variation: Make **HONEY BALLS**, or buy a real honeycomb and let older children eat pieces of it.

Make sure to give everyone goodie baskets with the same color and design. This will prevent squabbles and hurt feelings.

Brant Webster, Age 8

Games & Activities:

• Read appropriate books like THE TEDDY BEAR PICNIC, THE LITTLE BEAR SERIES, A BIRTHDAY CAKE FOR LITTLE BEAR, GOLDILOCKS AND THE THREE BEARS, and any of the BERENSTAIN BEARS books.

• Play **THE TEDDY BEAR PASS.** The children pass a bear until the music stops, just like musical chairs. The child with the bear is out and the game continues until only one child is left.

• Play **MUSICAL BEARS.** Use bear shapes cut from poster paper instead of using chairs and tape them in a circle on the floor. Begin with one less bear than there are children. Play something peppy like "Teddy Bear Picnic". Have the children step from bear to bear as you play. Each time the music stops, the child not safe removes one bear. The last child left standing on a bear is the winner.

• Go on a **BEAR HUNT.** The leader tells all children to sit cross-legged in a circle. They are to repeat everything the leader says and mimic all of the actions of the leader simultaneously.

LEADER: (children repeat after each line)
We're going on a BEAR HUNT!
Oh, Look!

Can't go around it.
Can't go under it. — Refrain
Can't go over it.
Gotta go through it.

Rub palms together in a swishing motion. Then pat hands on the floor and say:

We're going on a BEAR HUNT!
Oh, look!
I see a lake!
REFRAIN
Gotta swim across it.

Move arms in a swimming motion. Pat hands on the floor again and say:

We're going on a BEAR HUNT!
Oh, look!
There's a tall tree (or a mountain, hill, etc.)
REFRAIN
Let's climb up it!

Move arms in a climbing motion. When reaching the top, hold hands over brow as if you are looking far away and say:

Oh, look!
I see a cave!
Let's go down and see what is inside!

Climb down tree. (or mountain) Pat hands to walk to cave.
Slow patting beat down to say:

Oooo... it's cold in here!
I feel something warm...
I feel something furry...
It's a bear!

Pat your hands in a fast pace as if running and repeat motions
in reverse order very quickly, saying:

Up the tree (climbing motion)
Swim across the lake (swimming motion)
Through the grass (waving grass motion)
We're Safe!

For older children, you may add more obstacles as you wish. This game can be played from ages 3 on up.

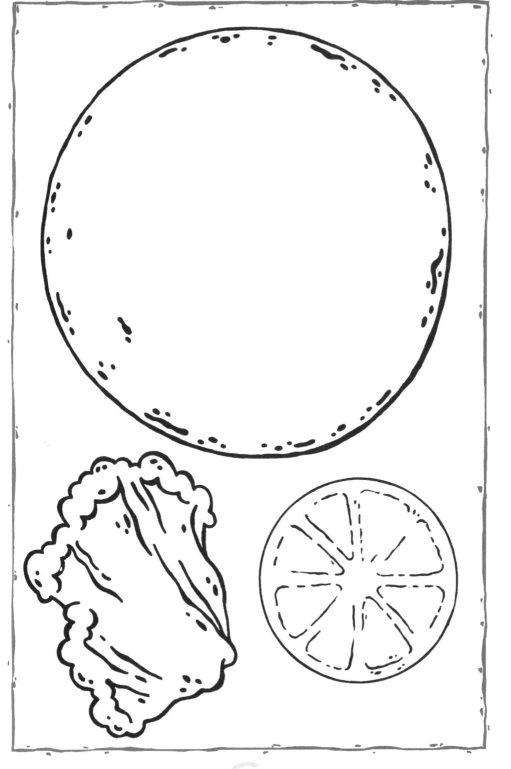

SOUTHWESTERN GET-TOGETHER

Invitations:

Cut the taco pattern out of brown construction paper or a heavy paper bag. Write party information on lettuce-shaped green construction paper and round tomato circles of red paper. Fold brown paper around the lettuce & tomato and tuck it in an envelope.

PAPEL PICADO

Decorations & Favors:

• Decorate with Mexican sombreros, piñatas, streamers, and brightly colored crepe paper.

• Hang PAPEL PICADO (pierced paper) around the room. These festive Mexican cutouts are easily made by folding tissue paper accordion style and cutting shapes from the folds. Unfold and tape to lengths of string.

• As children arrive, allow them to make tissue paper flowers and then use them to decorate the party room.

• Older children might enjoy real cactus plants in small pots which can be used as decorations and then taken home as favors.

Tissue Paper Flowers

Fold several layers of tissue paper accordion style and trim the ends in a semi-circular fashion. Twist a florist's wire around the middle of the tissue. Gently pull the layers of tissue paper up to form a tissue flower.

MENU

Tacos

Curly Taco Mix

Southwestern
Layer Dip & Chips

Giant Cookie

Innocent Margaritas

25

Children love tacos! Tacos are a good source of nutrition and they're fun to make!

Games & Activities:

• Have the following ingredients ready ahead of time so the children can make their own tacos.

TACO FILLING & shells   Sliced Black Olives
Chopped Tomatoes   Chopped Onions
Shredded Lettuce   Taco Sauce
Grated Cheddar Cheese   Sour Cream

• A game that smaller children enjoy is a **MEXICAN JUMPING BEAN RACE** where players jump from a start to a finish line.

• Make **NATIVE AMERICAN BRACELETS**. Cut an empty toilet paper tube down one side and then cut it into 1 1/2" tubes. Trim and round off the edges. Using aluminum foil, cover the tube, and flatten and smooth out the top. Color macaroni or any small pasta using one-half cup of rubbing alcohol and a few drops of blue food coloring. Drop in the macaroni and let set, then remove to dry. Allow the children to glue the dyed pieces of macaroni on the aluminum-foiled tube to create their own turquoise bracelet.

• Children can take turns trying to break candy-filled **PIÑATAS** with a plastic bat.

PAPER BAG PIÑATA

Cut brightly colored tissue paper into 3" strips. Cut into fringe leaving a 1" strip at the top. Glue these strips on a brown paper bag, letting the strips overlap. Cover the whole bag. Punch holes with a hole punch about 2" apart around the top of the bag. Thread the holes with string or yarn. Attach streamers to the bottom for a festive look. Fill with your favorite candy and tie it shut. Use a rolled up newspaper as a stick to hit and break open the piñata.

HANGER PIÑATA

Fill a plastic grocery bag with candy and hang from a coat hanger. Draw your favorite animal or character on butcher paper, large enough to cover the coat hanger and bag. Repeat for the other side of the piñata or draw a new picture the same size. Staple the two pictures back to back around the bag and coat hanger.

MAKE AHEAD PIÑATA

This is a project that you and your child can make a few days before the party. Cut several sheets of newspaper into thin strips. Blow up a balloon and tie it securely. Cover the entire balloon with newspaper strips dipped in starch or flour and water paste. Apply enough smooth layers of strips to make a solid covering on the balloon. Let this dry for a few days. Carefully cut a small opening in the top of the dry piñata and push wrapped candy into the opening. Use masking tape to cover the opening. Decorate the outside of the newspaper-covered balloon, using flowers, leaves, paper, etcetera.

YOU'RE INVITED TO AN
Old Fashioned Picnic

When

Where

Given by

OLD FASHIONED PICNIC

Invitations:

Copy the designed invitation provided onto red paper. For added fun, glue small plastic ants to each invitation!

Decorations & Favors:

• Pack lunches in small peach or produce baskets lined with colorful napkins. Tie a bow on the handle or around the basket, using strips of red gingham or calico.

• In the basket, include favors like inexpensive sunglasses, sample size suntan lotion, balls and jacks.

• Use a red gingham tablecloth to cover the picnic table or lay the tablecloth out under a nice shade tree for the children to sit on.

MENU

Oven Fried Chicken
Baked Beans
Biscuits
Sliced Cucumbers
& Tomatoes
Watermelon
Ice Cream
Toppings & Sauces
for Sundaes
Lemonade

Games & Activities:

• Play **WATER BALLOON TOSS**. Fill balloons with water. Divide the children into pairs. Each pair stands a few feet apart, facing each other. They toss a balloon to each other, backing up a little after each successful catch. The game continues until the balloon breaks.

FOR THE FOLLOWING RELAY RACES, DIVIDE THE CHILDREN INTO TEAMS.

EGG IN THE SPOON RACE

Give a tablespoon and a raw egg to each player. The players are to run from one point to another without dropping or breaking the egg.

CENTIPEDE RACE

Instead of tying only two children's ankles together as in a three-legged race, tie the entire teams' ankles together and watch these "centipedes" try to complete the race without falling down.

POTATO RELAY

In this race, the players run with a potato between their legs and attempt to drop it in a bucket placed at the finish line. Remember, no hands!

• Younger children enjoy active games like "Tag", "Red Light-Green Light", and "Red Rover".

• The picnic would not be complete without a game of **HORSESHOES**.

• Some other picnic games are a watermelon seed spitting contest, a tug-of-war, or a pie eating contest using paper plates covered with whipped cream or applesauce.

After the children are finished playing games, set out chocolate and vanilla ice cream along with various toppings, sauces, and sprinkles. Then let them at it!

Some topping suggestions:

HOT FUDGE SAUCE

BUTTERSCOTCH SAUCE

NUTS

CANDY

COCONUT

SPRINKLES

CHERRIES

WHIPPED CREAM

Here's an idea:
Purchase a plastic gutter and build a giant sundae for everyone to dig into!

You and your favorite doll
are cordially invited to come for tea.
Please come dressed in
Mom's high heels and jewelry.

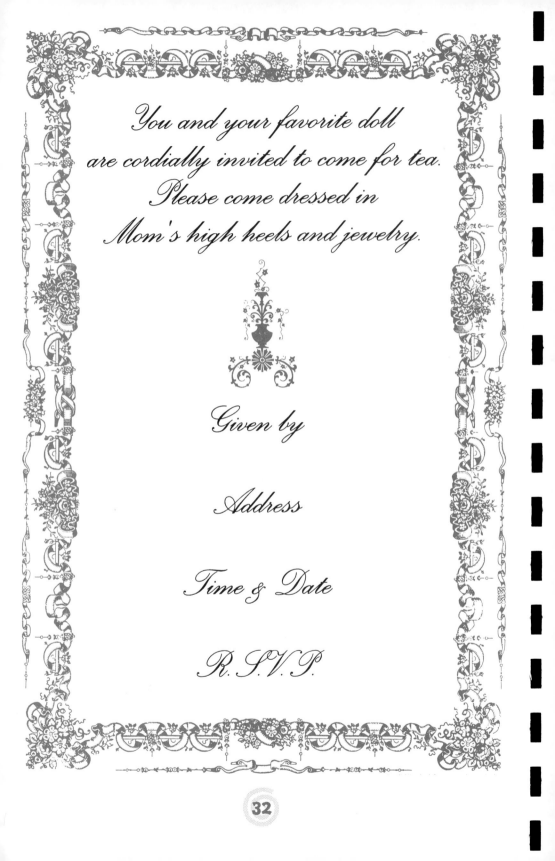

Given by

Address

Time & Date

R.S.V.P.

TIME FOR TEA

Amy Shuart, Age 11

Invitations:

Copy the formal invitation provided. Be sure parents realize that the girls are supposed to come dressed in their mothers' clothes.

Decorations & Favors:

• Sit dolls of all sizes on the front porch or stairs to greet the guests.

• Cover the table with a fancy lace tablecloth. Use china and crystal for older girls. Colored plastic plates and punch cups are fine for younger fingers. Set up a separate table with small play china for the dolls.

• Decorate with fresh flowers, candles, balloons, and pink streamers.

• Make place cards with pretty flower stickers. Have name tags for the dolls with both the doll's name and her "mother's" name printed on them.

• Buy inexpensive tea cups to use as favors. Serve the tea in them or fill them with mints and candy for the ladies to take home.

• Lip gloss, nail polish, barrettes, and hair ribbons also make wonderful favors. Give plastic baby bottles or rattles to the dolls.

MENU

Ham Biscuits

Veggie Tray/Dip

Strawberries
in Powdered Sugar

Scones & Jam

Petit Fours

Tea with
Sugar Cubes & Lemon

LADIES FASHION SHOW 12:30 PM

Games & Activities:

• Make **BONNETS** using straw hats, ribbons, dried or silk flowers, and lace. Most of these items can be purchased at a craft store.

• Award ribbons to the cutest, funniest, biggest, and smallest dolls, making sure that everyone gets something.

• Have a **FASHION SHOW** of the ladies' attire, with each lady describing her outfit.

• Making **PAPER DOLLS** is always fun. Have each child bring a picture of herself to be cut out and used as the face for her paper doll. The children can cut the dolls out of cardboard and then glue their own face to the doll. By using the doll as a pattern, they draw clothes and accessories on paper and cut them out.

• The perfect card game is "Old Maid". Place four girls at each card table and offer M&Ms and popcorn for munchies.

Here's an Idea: Mom and Dad can dress as butler and maid and serve the ladies' food on silver trays. (In several courses, of course!)

Sarah Stinson, Age 8

Beach Party

When

Where

Given by

BEACH PARTY

Invitations:

Copy the designed invitation provided or, for older children, write party details on a slip of paper and insert it into a washed clam shell. Secure the shell with a raffia tie and place into a small box for the mail or for hand delivery.

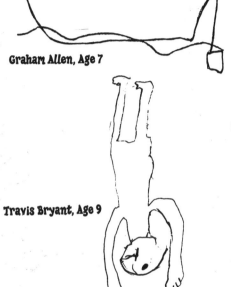

Graham Allen, Age 7

Travis Bryant, Age 9

Decorations & Favors:

• Cover the party table with a fish net. This can be found at a nautical gift shop or a marine supply store.

• Use the GELATIN FISHBOWL as a table centerpiece. Add seashells around the base of the bowl.

• Use beach towels for seating and beach umbrellas for shade.

• Beach balls make fun decorations, too.

• Use fish nets or onion bags for goodies and fill with "Go Fish" cards, fish shaped jelly candy, salt water taffy, frisbees, sunglasses, and water guns .

• Serve the food inside a frisbee lined with a paper plate. Food can also be served buffet style out of sand buckets with shovels.

Menu Variation:

• Have a large cooler or wheelbarrow filled with ice for canned drinks.

• Make a big splash by serving a 4'-6' submarine sandwich!

MENU

Tuna Sails

Fish Shaped Crackers

Skewered Fruit

Gelatin Fishbowl

Sailboat Cake

Frothy Seas

Morgan Warthan, Age 4

The Limbo is always a great Beach Party Game.

Games & Activities:

Indoor

• Make **HULA SKIRTS** to put on the children as they arrive. Cut long strips of greenbar computer paper and attach to waist-sized lengths of masking tape. Cover with another piece of tape. If computer paper is not available, tie long pieces of raffia to a waist-sized length of rope. The skirts can be tied on or safety pinned.

• Decorate sunglasses or picture frames with small shells, puff paints, jewels and paint markers.

• Make **TISSUE PAPER FISH**. Use two sheets of tissue paper placed on top of each other. Design a fish and cut out the pattern, back and front. Glue all edges together except the tail. Stuff with tissue and hang with a thread.

Here's an Idea:

For a winter party, turn the heat up in the house and have party guests wear their bathing suits under their winter coats. Use beach towels, balls and umbrellas as indoor decorations.

Outdoor

• Bubble-blowing and water balloons make fun outdoor activities.

• Set up small pools, Slip-and-Slides, and sprinklers to create an aquatic obstacle course.

• Have a water gun target practice and then play water gun tag. Make sure to have plenty of extra water guns, in case some break.

Outdoor or Indoor

• Have children fish for prizes. Cut fish out of construction paper and clip a paperclip to each one. Put a number on each fish. The numbers should correspond to numbered party favors. Use an old fishing pole and replace the hook with a magnet. Have each child cast the line into a plastic swimming pool or large bucket filled with the fish and pull out a fish. The child will receive the favor that has the same number as the fish he or she caught.

Julie Hatchett, Age 7

Print a fish!

Paint a real fish with thinned poster paint. Lay a piece of typewriter paper over the fish to create a fossil print. Print T-shirts by using fabric paint.

ADMIT ONE

to the

BIG TOP

Given by_____

Address_____
_____

Date_____

Time_____

UNDER THE BIG TOP

Invitations:

Copy the designed invitation onto brightly colored paper.

Decorations & Favors:

• Tie helium balloons to the bannisters and mailbox to identify the location of the party.

• Use a bouquet of balloons as a table arrangement. Use wild stuffed animals for decorations to delight the peanut gallery.

• Drape colored crepe paper from a light fixture outward to form a big top in the party room.

• Animal cookies in circus car boxes make perfect favors. If a clown is available, he can distribute rings, marbles, and gum from the large pockets in his costume.

• Rent a cotton candy machine, moon walk, dunking booth or snow cone machine to help create the carnival atmosphere.

Menu Variation:

If a meal is planned, this is a great time for hot dogs and all the trimmings.

MENU

Peanuts

Caramel Apples

Popcorn Clusters

Snowcones

Clownface Ice Cream

Ice Cream Cone Cupcakes

Polka Dot Punch

Games & Activities:

• Hire a clown to juggle, do balloon sculptures and pass out goodies. A good-hearted neighbor might be pressed into service for free.

•Paint **CLOWN FACES** on the children. All it takes is a steady hand, clown make-up and a little imagination.

• Try a **BEAN BAG TOSS**. Draw a large clown face on poster board and cut out the mouth. Make small square bean bags out of brightly colored fabrics. Give a lollipop or small candy bar to each child who is able to toss the bag through the clown's mouth.

• How about a **BALLOON SWEEP**? Use small brooms and have the party guests sweep their balloons from a starting line to a finish line. This game is harder than it sounds!

• Play **PEANUT PUSH**. The children pretend they are circus elephants and must push a peanut with their nose to a designated finish line without using their hands.

• Some other fun activities are ring toss, bobbing for apples, and bubble gum blowing contests.

• Have a **POPCORN RACE**. Punch a small hole in the bottom of a plastic party cup. Tie a knot in one end of a rubber band and thread it through the hole. Divide children into teams and place a cup on one child's foot from each team. Fill the cups with popcorn. Have buckets at the finish line for the popcorn to be dumped into. The children on a team take turns being the racer and filling the racer's cups. The first team to fill its bucket, wins.

Ben Hallissy, Age 8

YOU ARE INVITED TO A
PLAYBALL
SPORTS PARTY
IN HONOR OF OUR
MOST VALUABLE PLAYER

_____

GAME DAY

GAME TIME

PLAYING FIELD

PLAY BALL

Invitations:

Copy the designed invitation provided.

Decorations & Favors:

• When the children arrive, allow them to autograph the ball shaped cake with tubes of decorator frosting.

• Decorate with a team banner, pennants, pom-poms, and balloons in team colors.

• For each child, have a baseball cap filled with gum, sports balls, and baseball or football cards.

• Mom and Dad can be dressed as referees.

Bryan Barr, Age 8

MENU

Hot Dogs

Popcorn Clusters

Dill Pickles

Peanuts & Pretzels

Favorite Ball Cake

Soda Pop

Maintain parental control of the party by keeping a referee's whistle handy.

Games & Activities:

• For these games, divide the children into teams. To designate team players, have hats, T-shirts, or bandannas in 2 different colors. Hand these out at the door, alternating colors with every child.

VOLLEYBALL

Play volleyball with a beach ball.

CROQUET

Play as you would regular croquet, but use oranges or pinecones in place of the croquet balls.

BASEBALL

Play this game with a whiffle ball and a plastic bat.

FLAG FOOTBALL

Each player wears a flag or bandanna tucked under his or her belt. The game is played by pulling the other team's flags instead of tackling.

DRIBBLE BASKETBALL

Played as a relay, each team tries to make as many baskets as possible. Place tape on the ground to designate spots to dribble to and shoot from.

SLALOM SOCCER

Fill milk jugs with water and set up, five feet apart, in two rows. Each player takes a turn dribbling the ball with his or her feet through the rows of milk jugs and back again.

HOCKEY

Set up a goal and let each player take turns with a hockey stick. The object will be to shoot as many balls into the goal as possible in the time limit given. Use a whistle for starts and stops.

• Decorate visors, caps, water bottles or plastic megaphones.

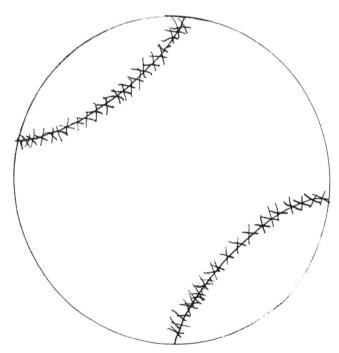

Jenny Barr, Age 11

WANTED

**Special Friends
to help celebrate
the Wild West
birthday
of**

_____

Address

Date

Time

WILD WEST PARTY

Invitations:

Copy the designed invitation onto parchment paper or tan colored paper.

Decorations & Favors:

• Use a calico cloth, bandannas, or a colorful blanket on the table and arrange assorted cowboy paraphernalia. Put a few daisies in a child's boot as a centerpiece.

• Water pistols are great cowboy favors.

• Western hats, sheriff's badges, and bandannas can be given as prizes for some of the games mentioned on the next few pages.

Erin Kane, Age 9

Menu Variation:

Serve BRANDED PANCAKES and Sausage Links. Barbecue chicken wings from a take out restaurant are an easy menu variation.

╼MENU╾
Bar-B-Que
Corn on the Cob
Coleslaw
Cowboy Cookies
Sheriff's Badge Cake
Ginger Ale

Games & Activities:

• This is the perfect party for **PONY RIDES**. Children enjoy feeding the pony as much as riding it, so have apples and carrots on hand. Have an instant camera loaded so that the children can take home pictures of themselves on the pony.

• Play **PIN THE BADGE ON THE SHERIFF**. For the sheriff's picture, trace the birthday person on butcher paper; cowboy hat and all. Get the children to fill in the features (with some discretion) and add a badge. The game is then played by the same rules as PIN THE TAIL ON THE DONKEY, using badges in place of tails.

• Make a **WESTERN VEST**. Cut arm and neckholes and a front opening in brown grocery bags. Decorate with markers, old buttons, feathers, yarn, and fringe made from more brown paper.

• Have a **LASSOING CONTEST**. Use a hula hoop to rope a wooden or spring rocking horse.

• Have an outdoor **BALLOON RACE**. Use water pistols to squirt balloons from a starting line to a finish line.

If a real pony is not available, have the children ride sock horses! Stuff the foot-end of socks and decorate with buttons, markers and yarn. The tips of old gloves make great ears. Tie the end of the sock around a dowel and Giddy Up!

DOUBLE R BAR   **RUNNING W RANCH**

• For the next two games, divide the party into two ranches or teams. Name one team the DOUBLE R BAR and the other team the RUNNING W. Brand the little ranch hands with their ranch's symbol, using a washable magic marker. Give sheriff's badges to the winning ranch. Don't forget to give some kind of prize to the losing ranch for being good sports!

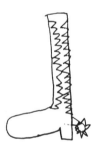

Lauren Hebert, Age 10

ROUND UP GAME

Pick a foreman from each ranch to be the leader. The foreman begins by tagging one player, who then joins hands with the leader who tagged him. The two of them try to tag two others. As soon as players are tagged, they are to join hands with the group that has tagged them. Only players on the end can tag. If a line can encircle one or more players completely, they are considered tagged. Each ranch tries to round-up the largest number of ranch hands!

GIDDY UP HORSEY RELAY

Each ranch hand gallops around a course on a stick horse or broomstick. Then he gives his horse to the next player in line. The first ranch to complete the race, wins.

Carter Joyce, Age 7

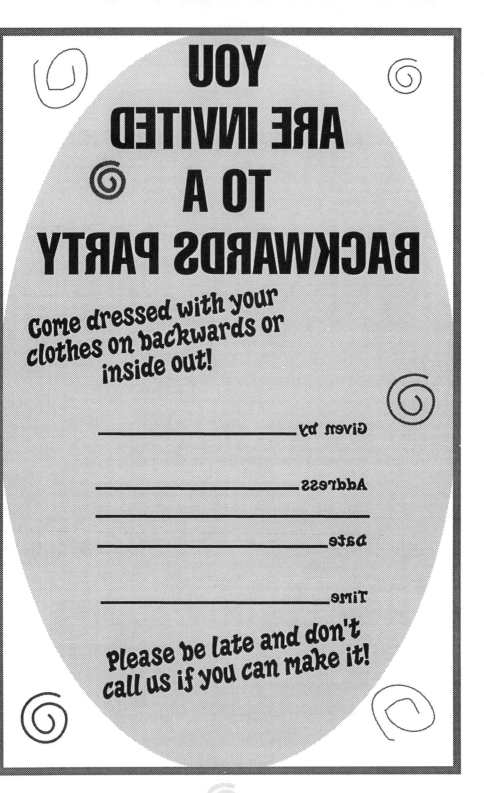

YOU
ARE INVITED
TO A
BACKWARDS PARTY

Come dressed with your clothes on backwards or inside out!

_____ Given by

_____ Address

_____

_____ Date

_____ Time

Please be late and don't call us if you can make it!

BACKWARDS PARTY

(title printed in mirror-reversed/backwards lettering)

Invitations:

Copy the designed invitation. You and your child can have some fun trying to fill in the party information backwards.

Decorations & Favors:

• Have a birthday cake with HAPPY BIRTHDAY written backwards.
• Use mirrors throughout the room.
• Turn the chairs away from the table and hang the pictures upside down.
• Decorate with beach balls and sand pails in winter or snowflakes and Christmas trees in summer!
• Place a vase upside down in the center of the table with flowers sticking out from under it. Have the plates and cups upside down and have the place settings reversed.

MENU

Morning:
Spaghetti

Afternoon:
Pancakes

**Serve cake
on top of ice cream**

Eat cake and ice cream, then the main course.

Games & Activities:

• Give out goodie bags and say "Goodbye" when the children arrive.

• Open presents first! The birthday child will love that idea most of all!

• Draw pictures with feet! Tape a large piece of paper to the floor. Children are to draw by holding markers between their toes. Have the names of easy-to-draw objects written on scraps of paper. The birthday child can pull the scraps out of a hat and the guests can try to draw them.

• Play **PIN THE DONKEY ON THE TAIL.**

• Fill a wide mouth jar with plastic spring type clothespins. Use a magnet on a string and try to get the most clothespins out of the bottle.

• Have a **RUN BACKWARDS RACE.**

• For more thrills, try a **THREE LEGGED RACE** with one partner forward and one partner backwards.

• Have a **SHOE SCRAMBLE.** All players remove their shoes and pile them in the middle of the room. At the signal, the children run to find their shoes and put them on the wrong feet.

Some "seasonal" Menu Suggestions:

Winter

Chicken Kabobs

Fruit Bowl

Popsicles
or
Ice Cream Cones

Summer

Chili

Corn Muffins

Hot Chocolate

MEET THE STAR OF STAGE AND SCREEN

We are having a
Hollywood Movie Party
to recognize the
legendary superstar

[   ]

You will be fashionable to arrive at

:

on

,

Our cinematic extravaganza is being held

at

 Everyone who is anyone will be there,
so come and join the stars!

BE A STAR

Invitations:

Copy the designed invitation provided or cut stars out of gold construction paper. Include all necessary information; feel free to use the same wording on the pre-printed invitation.

Decorations & Favors:

• Use movie posters for general decorations.

• Cut yellow stars from posterboard and use as place cards with guests' names written with metallic markers.

• Use confetti, stars, sequins and jewels scattered over a tablecloth for a glamorous effect.

• Top the table off with favorite movie theater candies and brightly colored streamers.

• Glitzy costume jewelry and movie star sunglasses make great favors.

• Purchase paper paint buckets from a hardware store and decorate with foil, star stickers, and ribbons. Fill with popcorn that can be eaten at the party or taken home.

• Discount movie coupons and autograph books also make good favors.

MENU

Party Pinwheels

Apple Slices with Dip

Fun-Flavored Popcorn

Video Cake

Shirley Temples

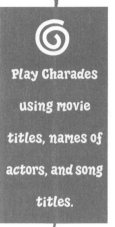

Games & Activities:

•Have **AUDITIONS**. This game is played like "Simon Says". One child is the director and others are actors. The director gives the instructions and the actors follow the instructions only if the director says "action" immediately after the instruction. If the director doesn't say "action" then the actors who followed that instruction are "out".

• **GATHER THE STARS** game is a good ice breaker, especially if all the guests don't know each other. Use plastic covered name tags with a star sticker added. If a guest catches another guest using the word "I", or any other chosen word, he or she can take the other guest's star. At the end of the party, or at a designated time, the person with the most stars wins.

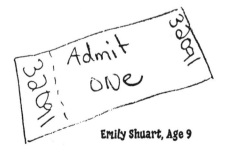

Emily Shuart, Age 9

• Make your own movie using a video camera. Film a performance of your little "stars". Divide the party into groups and suggest a topic to perform such as

CRAZY ADVERTISEMENT

MODERNIZE A FAIRY TALE

MAKE A NEW EPISODE OF YOUR FAVORITE TV SHOW

MAKE A MUSIC VIDEO

PUT ON A VARIETY SHOW

Small groups usually work better than large ones, especially with younger children. Allow a fixed rehearsal time and then start rolling!

Allow time at the end of the party for viewing and signing autographs.

Heather Lewis, Age 7

YOU ARE INVITED TO A MYSTERY PARTY!

SECRET DAY

SECRET TIME

SECRET PLACE

MYSTERY PARTY

Invitations:

Copy the designed invitation provided,
OR
Write the party information with lemon juice on paper. Print IRON ME with regular ink. When the invitation is ironed, the message mysteriously appears.

Decorations & Favors:

• Decorate a red paper table cloth with black cut-out footprints. As children arrive, they can fingerprint or handprint the table cloth with tempera paint to add a more puzzling effect.

• If this is a birthday party, arrange lettered cupcakes on the table. When in order, they would spell out HAPPY BIRTHDAY. Have them jumbled so that the children have to decipher the message!

• Decorate small white paper bags with question marks and fill with detective badges, magnifying glasses, disguises, flashlights, and magic tricks.

• When the guests arrive, have a jar filled with candies at the door and allow each guest a chance at guessing how many pieces of candy are in the jar. The winner gets to take it home.

Menu Variation: Blend a variety of candies into ice cream, serve in cups and let children figure out which different candies are in the ice cream.

MENU

Surprise Burgers

Mystery Salad

Cupcakes
with a Secret

Painted Punch

Games & Activities:

If your budget allows, have a magician come to perform!

• Play **DETECTIVE GAME**. Take something from each guest as he or she arrives at the party (without letting anyone else see). Number all of the items and place them on a tray. Let the children sit in a circle with the tray in the middle and have them deduce what item belongs to which guest.

• Another game children enjoy is **WHO'S WHO?**. Have each guest write a description of himself or herself. Prompt them by giving specific things to include such as where they were born, their best subject in school, how many siblings they have, or their favorite things. Read them out loud and have everyone guess who the person is that is being described.

• Prior to the party, obtain baby pictures of the guests. The more embarrassing the pose, the better. Number and display the pictures. Guests must identify the pictures. The one with the most correct answers wins.

• Play **MURDER**. One person is the District Attorney. He or she passes out cards. If playing cards are used, make the Jack of Spades be the murderer. No one should let anyone else see his or her card. The District Attorney turns out the lights or draws the drapes to darken the room and leaves. Everyone must get up and move to a different seat. The murderer "murders" someone (gently please - a tap on the shoulder will do) and the victim screams and drops to the floor. The District Attorney returns and must identify the murderer by asking questions, and only the murderer is permitted to lie.

When the District Attorney says "You are the guilty one!", the accused must show his or her card to prove his or her innocence or guilt. If the District Attorney cannot guess the murderer in three guesses, the game is repeated. If he or she does guess the murderer, then the murderer becomes the District Attorney for the next game.

• Go for a **MYSTERY RIDE**. Take the children on a ride to a mystery spot, such as a roller rink, bowling alley, or theater.

• Children love to decode messages. Make up an alphabet code using one letter to stand for another and write messages for each child; you could include their names and addresses. The children then can use the code to decipher their messages.

TOP SECRET
FOR YOUR EYES ONLY

A=T	J=S	S=N
B=O	K=Y	T=F
C=D	L=E	U=G
D=K	M=I	V=C
E=Z	N=P	W=J
F=U	O=W	X=H
G=R	P=A	Y=Q
H=X	Q=B	Z=L
I=M	R=V	

THE YOUNG SWASHBUCKLER

IS REQUESTING YOUR FINE PRESENCE AT A

PIRATE PARTY

SECRET LOCATION

DATE

TIME

AHOY, MATIES!

PIRATE PARTY

Invitations:

Copy the designed invitation onto
parchment paper, tan paper, or paper bags.
On the other side of the invitation, draw a
treasure map of your neighborhood, marking
an "X" over your house.

Decorations & Favors:

• Cover the table with a black tablecloth and scatter gold
chocolate coins on it.

• Line up the PIRATE SHIP SANDWICHES as a flotilla
centerpiece.

• Red and black balloons, maps, and a skull and
crossbones flag complete the pirate theme.

Clark Belote, Age 6

• Have a big treasure chest filled with striped shirts, fake
beards, pirate hats, and bandannas. Also include some
brass curtain rings with string tied through them to be
used as earrings. The children can transform themselves
into pirates as they arrive.

• Dip pennies in a mixture of 1/2 cup vinegar and 1/4
cup of salt. Use these shiny pennies as decorations or
favors.

MENU

Pirate Ships

Gold Coins

Walk The Plank Snacks

Treasure Chest Cake

Rootbeer
in Frosty Mugs

65

Games & Activities:

• Make pirate hats and black eye patches. Use black cardboard to make the pirate hat and decorate it with gold glitter and sequins. Create the eye patch using black cardboard and black elastic.

• The highlight of this party will be the **TREASURE HUNT**. The party guests are to be divided into two teams. Each team is given a starting clue. This clue leads to the next and so on. Try this with each team receiving the same clue but in different sections of the house or upstairs and downstairs. The last clue brings everybody to the refrigerator where the Treasure Chest Cake is waiting.

Clues:

Hello, Hello, are you there?
Pick up a clue close to your ear. (telephone)

Sometimes I'm cold, sometimes I'm hot,
I'm ready when you use a pot. (stove)

When you want warming, I'm surely it,
Where Cinderella liked to sit. (fireplace)

As you enter, please be neat.
This is where you wipe your feet. (doormat)

I wear a ring when I'm not clean.
Three men inside are sometimes seen. (bathtub)

I'm so tired, I could cry,
where, oh where, can I lie? (bed)

Keep my door shut, this is the rule,
It's the only way I keep my cool. (refrigerator)

• Play **WALK THE PLANK**. Lay a 2"x4" board on the floor. Children line up and take turns walking the length of the board without stepping off. The game can be made more challenging by having the children's hands tied loosely behind their backs and blindfolding them. The children could also try walking backwards or hopping on one foot.

• Play **X MARKS THE SPOT**, which is a variation of "Pin the Tail on the Donkey". Place a large drawing of a treasure map on the wall with a treasure chest indicated. Each child, blindfolded, marks an X, attempting to make it as near as possible to the treasure chest.

• Go on **CAPTAIN HOOK'S CROCODILE HUNT.**

Use a clock or kitchen timer that makes a loud, ticking sound.
This will be your "crocodile".
Hide it somewhere and have the children hunt for it.
The first child to find it wins.

FAVOR CHESTS

Cover shoe boxes with black construction paper. Decorate with gold rick-rack and
write each child's name on a box in metallic pen. These Favor Chests can be filled
with plastic jewelry, candy necklaces,
gold candy coins, and kaleidoscopes.

AROUND THE WORLD
P A S S P O R T

Name ———————————————————

for

——————————

Birthday

> Attach your photo here and bring this passport with you to the party.

Time————————

Date ———————————————————

Place ———————————————————

Reservations ———————————————

AROUND THE WORLD

Invitations:

Copy the designed invitation provided. As children arrive, attach it to the passport booklet.

Decorations & Favors:

• Create passport booklets by attaching several pages of plain paper together. Use the invitation each child brings back to the party as the cover for each book. The blank pages will be stamped as the children "visit" each country.

• Get stickers and/or stamps from different countries to put in passports.

• Decorate with flags and native items from around the globe, and use maps or posters from travel agencies.

• Put brochures out that are about the different countries that the children will be visiting.

• Purchase plain paper bags with handles, use stickers to decorate them to look like well-traveled suitcases, and then use them as the goodie bags.

• Food can be served in a central location with a menu identifying the country that the food is from.

MENU

England
Fish & Chips
(fish sticks & french fries)

Italy
Pasta Salad

China
Egg Rolls

France & Germany
Cream Puffs, Pretzels

Japan
Tea

Games & Activities:

• Set up stations, indoors or outdoors, which represent different countries. Each child should visit each country and pick up stickers, brochures, and maybe even taste some items or make things from that land. Large groups of children can be divided up and sent to different countries in pairs or smaller groups if needed.

China

Serve fortune cookies and make streamer kites. For the kite, use 6' lengths of colored crepe paper and attach with tape to a chop stick.

Japan

Make origami crafts from a kit.

Italy

Give your young Michaelangelos **PLAY CLAY (page 122)** and let them sculpt self-portraits or favorite pets.

England

Make a crown decorated with jewels! Use poster board to cut out crowns and wrap each in aluminum foil. Allow children to decorate with jewels and glitter paints. Then everyone can play "London Bridge Is Falling Down" in crowns!

France

Create a masterpiece to put on display when parents arrive by fingerpainting with hand lotion paint. Place a squirt of hand lotion and a drop or two of tempera paint on each piece of paper. The children will mix the color in as they paint. Give them a topic or just allow them to create their own masterpieces.

Spain

Make castinets from small jar lids. Spray paint in advance and punch a small hole in the middle of each. Thread a rubber band through each and attach on the back by putting a piece of a toothpick through the rubber band or knotting to secure. Then let children thread their thumb and middle fingers through the rubber bands and clank together.

Africa

Make fun paper mache' masks and play rhythm instruments.

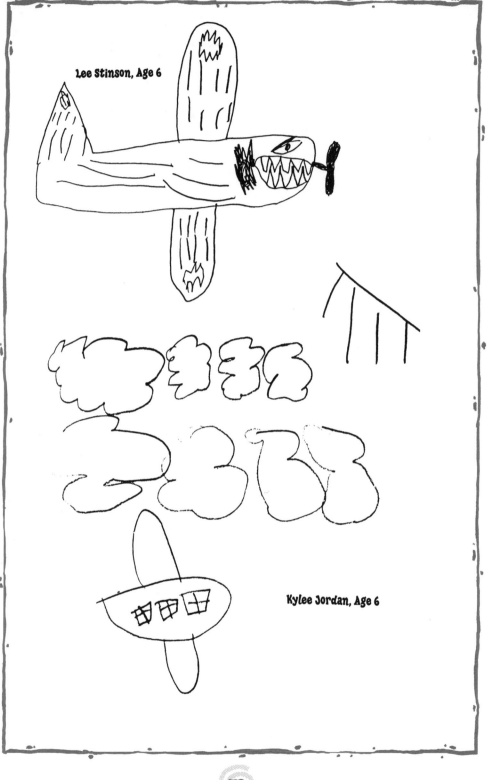

Lee Stinson, Age 6

Kylee Jordan, Age 6

COME FLY WITH ME

Invitations:

Write the party information on notebook paper and fold into a paper airplane.

Fasten Your Seatbelts for (name of child) Birthday Party

Destination: (address)

Arrival Time: (time that party will start)

Departure Time: (time)

For reservations: (your phone number)

Katie Johnson, Age 4

Decorations & Favors:

• Decorate the party room with airline posters and colorful kites. Hang an airplane mobile or inflatable plane from the ceiling.

• Obtain plastic wings, playing cards, etcetera from airlines. Ask for airsick bags to use as goodie bags for carry home favors.

• Kites and balsa wood planes also make good favors.

• Rent a moon walk .

MENU

Baked Potato Planes

Mixed Fruit
in a Plane Shaped
Watermelon

Airplane Cake

Propeller Punch

Parker Wingfield, Age 5

Games & Activities:

• Every pilot needs a **PARACHUTE**. Here's an easy one that is fun to make and can be done as an activity or as a take home favor. Tie 12" pieces of string to the four corners of a paper napkin. Add the pilot by tying a small plastic figure on the ends of the string. Toss the parachute in the air and watch it float down gracefully.

• Balsa planes can be purchased at hobby shops. Children can assemble them during the party and then have a plane flying contest.

• Allow the children to make and fly homemade kites. Serve refreshments while the glue on the kites is drying.

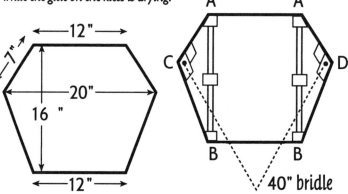

• Make a **SLED KITE** out of strong plastic garbage bags cut in these dimensions. Tape 2 sticks from A to B. Attach a 40" bridle at C & D. The bridle should be twice the width of the kite. Attach a flying string to the bridle. Tape on 3 or 4 rag tails for decoration.

• Make a **DIAMOND KITE** from a piece of heavy giftwrap paper about 20"x30". Fold the paper in half lengthwise. Unfold and refold in thirds the other way. With a ruler and a pencil, draw and cut out the diamond as illustrated. Fold back the four points of the diamond. Paste each point down on the wrong side of the paper, as shown. Wipe off the excess glue. Fold down a 1" border around the entire edge of the wrong side of the diamond.

Before pasting down the border, place a long piece of string in the fold. Join the string at the top. Don't fold points already pasted. Let string pass over them loosely. Cut two thin wood sticks 1" longer than the length and width of the kite. Notch the ends.

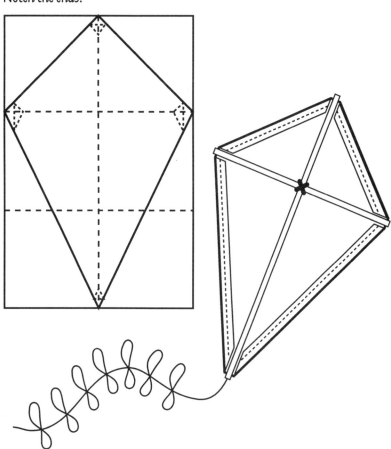

Place the sticks over the paper so that they cross. Tie with string at their intersection. Loop the string at the corners in the stick notches. Poke a hole in the paper at crossing. Slip a tie string through hole and tie to the crossed sticks. Tie rags to the bottom tip to form a tail.

COME TO AN
OLYMPIC PARTY

PLEASE COME DRESSED IN
SWEATS AND ATHLETIC SHOES!

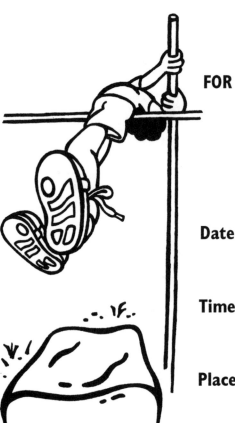

FOR

Date

Time

Place

OLYMPIC PARTY

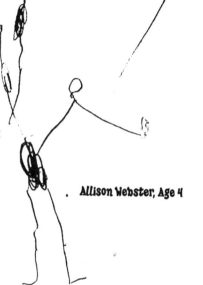

Allison Webster, Age 4

Invitations:

Copy the designed invitation provided.

Decorations & Favors:

• Decorate with red, white, and blue.

• Use a banner painted with the child's name and "Olympic Birthday" in large letters. The banner can also be done on a computer and then colored in with markers.

• Decorate with different countries' flags, streamers and balloons.

• Play some Olympic music as guests arrive and are playing games.

• Put paddle balls, jump ropes, stopwatches, and gold medal candies in paper bags and add red, yellow and orange tissue paper for flames to give as favors.

MENU

Pizza Casserole

Garlic Bread

Tossed Salad

Champion Brownies

Award Winning Punch

Take photos or a video of the children receiving their medals.

Games & Activities:

• Award ribbons only to the winners of the following games, or give a particular color ribbon to all of the participants in each game. For example, everyone who played in the "Track Race" gets a red ribbon.

Track Race

Play with 2 teams as a relay. Each player runs up, rolls a dice and races back to his or her line doing the activity that matches the number on the list. (Prepare a list of numbers from 1-6 and an activity for each. For example, 1. Walk backwards, 2. Skip, etcetera.)

Javelin Shoe Throw

Everyone stands in a large circle facing out. The players throw their shoes over their backs and then race to be the first to put them on. Another Javelin throw can be done using straws or blowing the paper off the straws.

Shot Put

Using a coin placed at the edge of a table, each player takes a drinking straw and in a designated time (i.e. 20 seconds) tries to blow his or her coin as far across the table as possible.

Discus Ring Toss

Children attempt to knock over an empty milk carton by tossing a frisbee at it. Give each child three chances.

Obstacle Course

Use a stopwatch to time the children and encourage crowd cheers as each child goes the distance.

1. Crawl through a tube or tunnel structure.

2. Walk the ropes by laying a 5' long string on the ground. Using binoculars turned upside down, look through them to walk the straight line.

3. Jump over three sticks laid 2 feet apart.

4. Roll on the ground to a certain spot.

5. Crawl on all fours to a tricycle.

6. Ride the tricycle 15 feet to cross the finish line.

Another Team Sport

Try playing soccer with a balloon!

Awards Ceremony

Use a sturdy box or crate decorated with the Olympic symbol as the stage. Give every child a medal for his or her special achievement. For example, the child who tried the hardest, was the best sport, and was the strongest.

HEARTS CONTENT

Invitations:

Make heart-shaped invitations with your youngster and decorate to your heart's content!

OR

Cut hearts about 5" tall out of poster board and punch holes about 1/4" around the outer edge. Using about 30" of red or pink ribbon, start at the top of the heart and weave the ribbon through the holes. End by tying a bow in the center. Write the invitation plans in pink or red ink to match the ribbon.

Decorations & Favors:

• Make paper hearts of all sizes and hang them from various lengths of thread.

• Make place cards using a pink or red ink pad. Press a thumb into the ink and then on to the card at a slight angle. Make a heart by stamping again at the opposite angle. Write guest's name in coordinating ink.

• Use fresh flowers for the table and add wooden hearts on dowels or paper hearts on pipe cleaners to the vase.

• A heart shaped sponge dipped in fabric paint can be used to decorate the tablecloth and goodie bags.

• Place some of the favors in a small margarine tub at the center of a sheet of foil. Put tissue around the base of the tub to resemble a "kiss" shape. Gather the corners together and twist into the shape of a candy kiss with a paper strip in the top with the name of the guest.

MENU

Heart Pizza

Hugs & Kisses

Hearts Galore Parfait

Double Heart Cookies

Happy Hearts Cake

Sweetheart Strawberry Daquiris

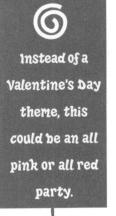

Games & Activities:

•Have **BALLOON MUSIC.** Start the music and toss several balloons in the air. The object of the game is for the children to keep the balloons in the air while dancing to the music.

• Another fun game is the **BALLOON POPPING DANCE.** Each guest ties a balloon around his or her ankle. As the children dance, they try to break other children's balloons with their feet while trying to protect their own balloons. Anyone who still has a balloon at the end of the song definitely deserves a prize!

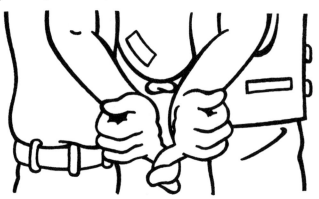

• **THE LINKING OF THE PINKIES.** Divide children into pairs and have them turn back to back and hook their pinkie fingers together. Place a balloon between their backs. Each pair of children has to lower themselves until seated on the floor and then get back up without breaking the pinkie link, dropping the balloon, or breaking it.

• Play **WHO AM I?** Each child is given a paper heart on which he or she is to write a favorite color, movie, book, food, animal, and then finally his or her name. All hearts are to be put in a box and the hostess reads each clue aloud (leaving off the name). Guests then guess who is being described by writing their answers down secretly. The child with the most correct answers wins.

• **THE SWEETEST STORY.** Pass a bowl of conversation hearts around and have each child take five. The hostess begins telling a story and each child adds a few lines. At each child's turn, he or she must use the words from one of the candy hearts. Go around the circle five times until each heart has been used. The sillier the story, the more fun!

Katelyn Lowery, Age 9

Please join us for a
spring
Celebration!

At the home of

When

Where

EGGS, EGGS, AND MORE EGGS!

Invitations:

Copy the designed invitation provided, or write the invitation on colored paper and put into a plastic egg tied with ribbon.

Decorations & Favors:

• Use the BUNNY CAKE as the table centerpiece.

• Create an Easter tree. Use a real tree branch and decorate with green paper leaves and popcorn for blossoms. Place your Easter tree in a flower pot filled with rocks and cover it with Easter grass. Hang plastic eggs from the branches and scatter dyed eggs around the base.

• The EGG NEST TREATS can be placed at each child's seat.

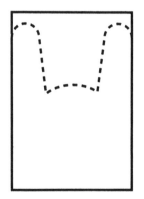

Bunny Bags

Cut a white lunch bag as shown in the diagram. Staple the ears together. Lay it flat and decorate the bunny's face. Add a cotton ball tail to the back for the final touch. Children will love these, especially when they are filled with special treats!

MENU

Egg Shaped Sandwiches

Carrot Sticks & Dip

Celery
with Peanut Butter
or Cream Cheese

Egg Nest Treats

Bunny Cake

Pink Lemonade

Jessica Lee, Age 9

Games & Activities:

• **EGG ROLL**. Each guest gets a hard-boiled egg and must roll it across the room with his or her nose.

• **JELLY BEAN EXCHANGE**. Give each child a dozen jelly beans. The object of the game is to get as many of one color as he or she can by trading. Set a timer for 3 minutes and let the game begin!

• **EASTER HAT RELAY**. Set up two tables at one end of the room. On each table place an assortment of hats. Divide the children into teams and have a relay. Each child must run to the table and put on each hat. Then he or she must parade around the table. The child removes the hats and returns to tag the next team member. The first finished team wins.

• **EGG-IN-THE-HAT**. Place a hat upside down across the room. Mark a line for the players to stand on and let them see how many eggs they can throw in the hat. Use plastic eggs or individually wrapped candy eggs that can be distributed later.

• **FEATHER-UP**. Use a feather and a stopwatch to see how long the children can keep a feather in the air. This can be done in groups holding hands. The group with the longest time wins.

• **BUNNYTAILS**. Give each child a small bowl, a straw, and the same number of cotton balls. Use the straw to suck up the cotton balls and put them in the bowl. The first child to finish is the winner.

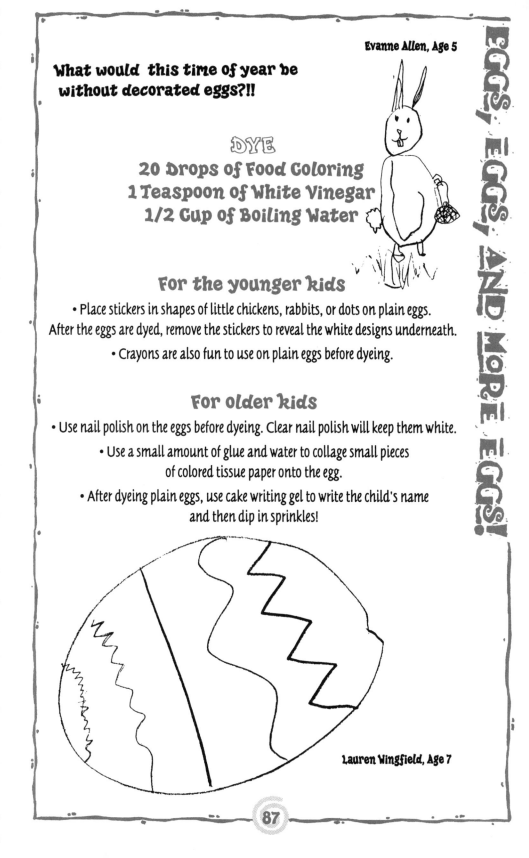

Evanne Allen, Age 5

What would this time of year be without decorated eggs?!!

DYE
20 Drops of Food Coloring
1 Teaspoon of White Vinegar
1/2 Cup of Boiling Water

For the younger kids

• Place stickers in shapes of little chickens, rabbits, or dots on plain eggs. After the eggs are dyed, remove the stickers to reveal the white designs underneath.

• Crayons are also fun to use on plain eggs before dyeing.

For older kids

• Use nail polish on the eggs before dyeing. Clear nail polish will keep them white.

• Use a small amount of glue and water to collage small pieces of colored tissue paper onto the egg.

• After dyeing plain eggs, use cake writing gel to write the child's name and then dip in sprinkles!

Lauren Wingfield, Age 7

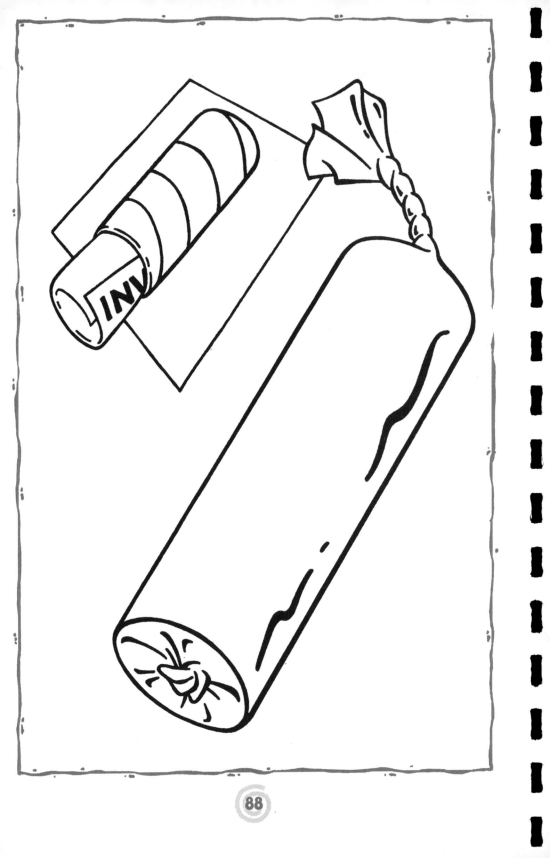

PATRIOTIC PARTY

Jeff Ostendorff, Age 8

Invitations:

Make invitations that look like firecrackers out of 6" cardboard tubing covered with red tissue paper. Write the party information with red ink on white paper and insert into the firecracker before gathering the tissue at each end and twisting or tying. Hand deliver .

Decorations & Favors:

• Unfurl "Old Glory" and line the walkway with small American flags.
• Decorate the patio with red, white and blue crepe paper.
• Use a red and white checked tablecloth. Fold red bandannas
and tie them around picnic silverware.
• Flags make good party favors.
• For a table arrangement, arrange red carnations, white daisies, and blue bachelor's buttons in a watermelon instead of a vase. Remove a 5" shallow plug and insert the flowers. Add firecrackers made from cardboard tubes topped with construction paper cones and covered with aluminum foil. Mount these in the melon with balloon sticks.

MENU
BBQ Chicken

Potato Salad

Roasted Corn

Fruit Pizza

Tasty Lemonade

Menu Variation: Have store bought hamburgers and hot dogs and RED, WHITE AND BLUE POPS.

Travis Pittman, Age 9

Make festive T-shirts or visors using star-shaped sponges, paints, and jewels.

Games & Activities:

• Try **ORANGE PASS RELAY**. Players form two lines and pass an orange down the line from chin to chin without using their hands.

• **RING TOSS**. Use 9 dowels decorated with patriotic colored streamers as the scoring poles. Set them up in 3 rows, 3 in each row, spaced 2' apart. Make rings by taping paper plates together and cutting circles out of the center. Each team gets 3 plates, and each team member gets 3 chances to score. A ring that lands around the closest poles is 10 points; a ringer in the middle is 20 points, and a ringer in the farthest row is 30 points.

• Do an **EGG TOSS**. Provide plastic aprons to protect clothing. Pair up the guests and have them toss a raw egg back and forth, while increasing the distance between each other with each throw.

• Hide little paper flags around the yard and have children find them.

• Play **BALLOON BRIGADE**. Each team assembles in single file with the first player in each line holding a balloon. When the whistle blows, each lead player passes the balloon between his or her legs to the next person in line. The recipient in turn passes the balloon overhead to the next person. The balloon is passed alternately between players' legs and heads all the way down the line. When the last person gets the balloon, he or she races to the front of the line and the balloon pass resumes. The relay continues until the first player regains position at the front of the line and pops the team balloon.

Patriotic Hats

Use a two-ply sheet of flat newspaper. Make the brim by measuring 3 1/2"
from the bottom of the sheet, mark it, then fold along the line and flatten
the fold. Paint the brim blue with acrylic or tempera paint and let dry. Then
paint broad red and white stripes on the flip side of the newspaper and let
dry. Next, cut star shapes from white construction paper and glue onto the
hat. Fit the hat by wrapping the brim (painted side out) securely around
the head and tape where needed. Use scissors to fringe the top of the hat,
making cuts that extend about halfway down the cylinder.

Bike Parade

Have piles of crepe paper streamers, tin cans, playing cards, balloons, ribbons,
stickers,etcetera.Give the guests plenty of time to decorate their bicycles or tricycles.
Then the host child leads the group around the block or up and down the street in
a parade. Carry a portable radio for music to ride by. You could also play "Red Light-
Green Light" on bikes. Have the guests line up on their bikes at the starting line.
Have someone at the finish line as a policeman with a green and a red flag. When
the green flag is up, children can ride. When the red flag is up they must stop. The
first one to the finish line wins and is the policeman for the next round.

SOME OF THE COOLEST
MONSTERS ANYWHERE
ARE GETTING
TOGETHER TO SHARE
SOME SCARE;
WEAR A GOOD
COSTUME AND WE'LL
SEE YOU THERE!

HALLOWEEN PARTY

WHEN

WHERE

GIVEN BY

PUMPKIN PATCH

Invitations:

Copy the designed invitation provided.

Decorations & Favors:

• Line the driveway with helium-filled black and orange balloons. Tie the strings to a garden hose to keep them all at the same height.

• Place Jack-O-Lanterns all around the party room and drape orange and black crepe paper everywhere.

• Give the JACK-O-LANTERN TREATS from the menu as favors and include small flashlights that can be used while trick-or-treating.

• Haunted hands are also good as favors. Put candy corn in the tips of clear plastic gloves, then fill them with popcorn and tie with a black ribbon.

• Make spider ice cubes by freezing small plastic spiders in ice cube trays. Serve in soft drinks or juice.

Menu Suggestion: Serve the GOBLIN'S GOOP in an Orange Jack-O-Lantern. Cut the top off of an orange and remove the fruit with a spoon. Carve a face in each orange and fill with the goop.

MENU

Spider Sandwiches

Goblins Goop

Jack-O-Lantern Treats

Ice Cream Pumpkins

Jack-O-Lantern Cake

Witches Brew

Decorate mini-pumpkins with markers and shapes cut out of colored paper.

Games & Activities:

• Hang a large sheet of butcher paper at child level on the wall. As the children arrive, have them draw a picture on the butcher paper of what they think they look like in their costume.

• It wouldn't be Halloween without a **COSTUME JUDGING CONTEST**. Give a prize to everyone in a different category. For example, scariest costume, funniest costume, or most colorful costume.

• Play **DRAW-THE-FACE-ON-THE-PUMPKIN**. Cut pumpkins out of orange construction paper. Each child is blindfolded and led to his or her pumpkin at an easel. He or she draws a Jack-O-Lantern face with a marker. All of the children will get a good laugh when the blindfold is removed!

• Play **WITCH AND BLACK CAT**. Sit the children in a circle. The birthday child is the first "witch" and leaves the room. A child in the circle is given a stuffed black cat or black cat silhouette to hide in his or her costume. When the witch returns, she tries to find her cat. As she walks around the circle, the closer she gets to her cat, the louder the children meow, until she finds her cat. The children take turns being the witch and hiding the cat.

Here's an idea: Adapt the **JUNGLE JUMBLE** on page 18 to Halloween themes.

Justin Russell, Age 6

Jason Micco, Age 6

Matthew Martin, Age 5

Jenny Feild, Age 9

Hanukkah

is a celebration of the Jewish revolt against the cruel Syrian King Antiochus and their victory over his mighty armies. It also celebrates the restoration and rededication of their Holy Temple in Jerusalem. Hanukkah is sometimes called The Festival of Lights in memory of the miracle that happened during the rededication. The only holy oil to be found for the eternal lamp was enough for one day of light, but it burned for 8 days, starting on the 25th day of the Jewish month of Kislev.

Please Spin By:

_____
is having a
Hanukkah
Celebration
time:
date:
address:

HANUKKAH CELEBRATION

Invitations:

Make paper dreidel shaped invitations using the illustration on page 96 as a guide. Draw a dreidel on thin cardboard, cut it out and use it as a template to make the invitations. Fold the sides over and decorate. Write the party information on the inside.

Decorations & Favors:

• Cut a long strip of Hanukkah wrapping paper and use as a runner on the table.

• Display all of your menorahs and dreidels.

• Set out bowls of gelt and other candies.

• Hang blue, white, silver and gold streamers around the party area. Tape colorful cut outs of dreidels, candles, and Stars of David to the streamers.

• Gelt Banks are a fun and easy favor for the children. Cover square tissue boxes or coffee cans with construction paper. Children can decorate using small coins, left-over Hanukkah paper, ribbons, crayons, and markers. Cut out a small hole at the top of the box to put gelt, pennies, or other small treasures into the bank.

Shin

Gimmel

Nun

Hay

Menu Variation: For younger children, serve white grape juice or apple juice to prevent stains.

MENU

Potato Latkes and Applesauce or Sour Cream

Doughnuts

Hanukkah Cookies

Grape Juice

Games & Activities:

•**PAPER MACHE DREIDELS**. Have your children help you make these several days in advance so they will be dry and ready to be painted when the party guests arrive. Cut 1 1/2" sections of empty paper towel or toilet paper tubes. Bend the small sections to make them into a square shape. Put masking tape over the open sides and poke a slightly sharpened dowel through the taped ends. Dip strips of newspaper into a mixture of equal parts flour and water, wiping off excess as you pull the paper out of the mixture. Apply the paper to the body of the dreidel. Allow to dry at room temperature or dry in the oven for a few hours on "warm". Have paints, glitter, etcetera ready for the guests to decorate their dreidels. Provide old shirts as smocks.

The Dreidel Game

Give each child an equal amount of candy gelt, pennies or jelly beans. They each put 2 into a central container and then take turns spinning the dreidel. If the dreidel lands on NUN, the player gets nothing. If it lands on GIMMEL, the player gets everything in the container. HAY means the player gets half of what is in the container and SHIN means the player has to pay a candy or a penny. Let the children play for only a certain amount of time. The child with the most at the end of the game is the winner.

• Make **SHORT-CUT DREIDELS** by cutting small squares out of construction paper and decorating. Poke small dowels or toothpicks through the center.

• **A STAR OF DAVID PICTURE FRAME MAGNET** is great for children to make and then take home as a present for someone else. Using wooden ice cream sticks and glue, make two triangles, then put the two triangles together to form the star. Attach a small magnet to the back and embellish the front with gold trim, sequins, buttons or markers. A photo can be placed in the center of the star.

• Have the party guests design their own **FABRIC MENORAH**, which can be lit each day of Hanukkah. The children draw their own pattern of a menorah on paper, or you can supply one. The pattern is then used to cut the menorah from any type of fabric. Candles and any other decorative motif can also be cut from fabric. Glue the Menorah to a felt background. Cut flames for the candles from another color felt and use them to "light" the Menorah. The felt flames will stick to the felt background.

The Shamash
is the ninth candle on the Menorah. It is used to light the other 8 candles; it should be higher or lower than the others.

Handprint Menorahs

Small children will love to make these. They trace around four fingers on each hand (not the thumb) and then draw in the ninth candle. By adding the base and the flames, they have a personalized Menorah!

snowflake patterns for invitation

CREATIVE CHRISTMAS

Invitations:

Using a cookie cutter, trace gingerbread boys onto coarse sandpaper. Glue on felt eyes, mouth, and buttons. Cut them out and paste on a note card or post card and include party plans. Instruct the children to come in play clothes or to bring smocks to cover nice outfits. Ask that each child bring a gift to include in a gift exchange or to donate to a needy group.

OR

Cut small snowflakes out of white paper and glue onto blue note cards so that the pattern shows through. Write the appropriate information on the inside.

Decorations & Favors:

• Since the house is already decorated for Christmas, no other decorations are needed.

• As children arrive, have them choose name tags made of construction paper. Make the name tags in the shape of trees, candy canes or stars. Have as many name tags as there are spaces at each activity table.

• Set up card tables for the craft activities and cover them with colored plastic table cloths. Label the tables with the corresponding name tag symbol: red-candy cane, green-tree, gold-star.

MENU

Popcorn

Pretzels & Nuts

Peppermint Ice Cream

Christmas Tree Cake

Cinnamon Cider

Hot Chocolate

Games & Activities:

• Purchase miniature Christmas trees and decorate with tiny items. For example, use spray-on snow and decorate with gold-wrapped candy kisses. Use wrapping paper as a tree skirt.

• Have Christmas cookies made in advance. Let the children decorate them with tube frosting and sprinkles. This "food activity" can be eaten at the party or taken home as favors.

• Make Christmas sweatshirts. The children can decorate plain sweatshirts with puff paints, sequins, and iron-on appliques with adult assistance.

Apple Santa Favors

Make one of these Santas ahead of time and display at one of the craft tables as an example for the children to follow. For arms and legs, stick toothpicks into apple, then push large marshmallows onto the toothpicks. Add small gumdrops for mittens and licorice bits for feet. Stick more toothpicks in the top of the apple and push cotton balls on to them to make Santa's beard. Another toothpick and marshmallow in the top/center of the apple will be the head, with cloves for eyes. On the top of the head, make a gumdrop and miniature marshmallow hat. Finish your Apple Santa Favor with gumdrop buttons and a licorice whip belt.

• The holidays are a wonderful opportunity to let children experience giving to those in need. Invite your party guests to bring canned goods for your local foodbank, or a toy to be given to charity. Some of the crafts made during the party could be donated to a community tree, hospital, or nursing home.

Gingerbread Houses

Assemble gingerbread houses ahead of time using graham crackers and tubes of white decorator frosting. Have lots of frosting, candies, mints, etcetera on hand for the children to finish off these yummy masterpieces.

A Kwanzaa Celebration–
The Karamu Feast

Kwanzaa is the African-American cultural holiday founded by Dr. Maulona Karenga and is celebrated from December 26 through January 1. It is unique in that it is not a religious, political, or heroic celebration, but is a cultural one. Kwanzaa is based on seven principles, called the **Nguzo Saba**, each one being celebrated on an individual day.

These principles are:

Umoja- Unity

Kujichagula- Self-Determination

Ujima- Collective Work and Responsibility

Ujamaa- Cooperative Economics

Nia- Purpose

Kuumba- Creativity

Imani- Faith

A special feast called **Karamu** is held on the sixth day of Kwanzaa.

KWANŽAA

Invitations:

• Make a **bendera** using construction paper and a wooden dowel. The bendera is a flag created by Marcus Garvey for African-Americans. It consists of three strips of construction paper with the bottom green strip representing the African land and the hopes and dreams of African- Americans. The black strip in the middle stands for the people and the unity and togetherness they share. The red strip on top represents the blood shed by Africans. On the back of the flag, glue a white piece of paper. Write all the party information there and decorate with examples of African symbols and fabrics, such as Kente cloth.

Decorations & Favors:

•Decorate the room in an African motif that uses a black, red, and green color scheme using paper chains and balloons in the three colors, African cloth, handmade flowers, sculptures, artifacts, or art made by African Americans.

• A table should be placed in the center of the room. Centered on the table should be the **mkeka** (placemat). A **kinara** (candleholder) with seven candles, called the **Mishumaa Saba**, is placed on the mkeka. The candles should be in the following order: 3 red candles on the left side, followed by the black candle in the center, and three green candles on the right side. The **kikomba cha umoja** (unity cup) is placed in front of the kinara, facing the side where the candles will be lit. A large basket or cornucopia filled with fruits and vegetables to represent the harvest, called the **mazao** is also placed on the table. In addition, **vibunzi** (ears of corn) for each child in the family, in the hope for the future, are placed on the table.

MENU
Kwanzaa Spicy Chicken

Tossed Salad

Cheesy Rice Balls

Fruit Salad

Karamu Cookies

Games & Activities:

• Make a **MKEKA**. Cut a 16" x 36" piece of black bulletin board paper and fold in half. Cut parallel lines (equal distances apart) to within 2 inches of the ends of the paper. Unfold the black paper and using red and green 2" wide strips of construction paper, weave the paper strips, alternating colors, through the slits. When all the strips have been woven, glue the ends of the strips to the black paper.

• Make **AFRICAN STATIONERY**. Use red or green paper with matching envelopes. Glue strips of beautiful African fabric along the top, sides, or bottom of the paper and also to the bottom edge of the back side of the envelopes. Tie with twine or a pretty ribbon. Makes a great **Zawadi**(Kwanzaa gift)!

Kwanzaa Booklet

For each booklet the supplies needed are :

White paper in the following sizes- 5 1/2" x 8 1/2", 6 1/2" x 8 1/2", 4 1/2" x 8 1/2"

red and green curling ribbon

red, green and black crayons

Fold paper, hole punch, and tie with curling ribbon bow as shown in diagram. In the reflections section, children record all the good things that they have experienced in the past year. The goals section is to record ways in which next year can be even better. The booklet can then be decorated with African symbols.

• Make a **HARVEST BASKET.** Spray paint small baskets or containers black. Provide red and green apples and red and green curling ribbon. Using foot-long lengths of curling ribbon, tie a bow around the stem of each apple. Place apples in baskets.

• **KARAMU COOKIE DECORATING.** Bake the Karamu cookies as directed in recipe. Using red, yellow, green, purple, and black food colorings to tint the frosting, "paint" the cooled cookies using African symbols and patterns.
Use **kuumba** (creativity)-be creative and design original patterns.

ADDITIONAL PARTY THEMES

ANIMAL

If your child really loves a certain type of animal, use it as the theme of a memorable party. Instead of buying printed table decorations, use plain ones that you and your child have decorated with stickers or crayons. Decorate a cake by tracing a picture of the animal on waxed paper and following the directions for the Sheriff's Badge Cake.

BACKYARD ART SHOW

Set up stations throughout your backyard stocked with paper and supplies for different projects. Some ideas for projects are painting at easels, making collages with old magazines, and creating colorful abstract pictures with tissue paper. Children also enjoy straw painting. This is done by placing a spoonful of paint onto a piece of paper and then blowing it into designs with a straw. Display all of the artwork on the easels, tables and a clothes line and award ribbons to everyone. Parents will enjoy touring the exhibit when they come to pick up their children.

BALLET

Invite your guests to come dressed in their leotards and tights (or sweat pants and shirt). Make tutus with netting and ribbon from a fabric store. (The salespeople at the store can help you if you are unsure about how to make them.) Hire a ballet teacher or have an older neighborhood child teach everyone ballet steps. There are also video tapes available for rent that teach ballet moves. Provide ballet music such as the Nutcracker Suite or Swan Lake for dancing. At the end of the party, put on a performance for the parents to watch before they take their children home.

BEAUTY PAGEANT

Have the girls come dressed in fancy dresses or in one of their mother's old gowns. Fix their hair, give makeovers and paint their nails. Give each girl a sash with the name of a state or country on it. They can pretend to be contestants in a beauty pageant and walk a runway for judging. Of course, the birthday girl is the winner and receives a crown. All others are the runners up and receive some sort of favor. Teenage girls make great helpers for this party.

BUBBLES & BALLOONS

Blow up balloons and write the party information on them, then deflate and send them as invitations. Decorate with balloons everywhere. Have shallow pans of bubble solution ready for blowing bubbles. To make homemade bubble solution, combine 1/2 cup dish detergent, 1 1/2 cups cold water and 10 drops glycerin, which can be purchased at a drug store. Use fun objects such as fly swatters, badminton racquets, empty strawberry baskets, and coat hangers bent in different shapes to make bubbles in all shapes and sizes.

CHARACTER

Have children come dressed as characters from their favorite classic book, or center the party around your child's favorite story. Have easy costumes ready for the children to dress in as they walk in the door. For instance, for a Three Musketeers party, provide big hats with paper plumes, fake mustaches and beards, tunics and pretend swords. For **Little Women**, provide full long skirts, gloves, and curls made out of yellow, brown, red, or black curling ribbon and attach to the girls' hair with bobby pins.

CHRISTMAS CAROLING

Make a snowman cake using an eight inch round cake for its head and a nine inch round cake for its body. Frost it white and decorate it with assorted candies. Serve hot chocolate and cider. Make small booklets of Christmas carols, leaving room for the children to illustrate them. Jingle bells and flashlights can be used during the caroling and will make good party favors.

COLOR

Have a party featuring your child's favorite color. Have the birthday child and party guests wear the color. Serve foods that are different shades of that color and give favors that are that color. Play games like "I Spy" using the color and have a scavenger hunt to find the appropriately colored items.

FIRE TRUCK

A Dalmatian cake is great fare for this party. Frost either a plain cake or a marble cake with white frosting and then use black frosting to make spots. Coloring books and small books about fire trucks placed inside firemen's hats can be used as favors. Set up a firemen's obstacle course. If possible, arrange a trip to your local fire station.

FIRST BIRTHDAY

For your baby's first birthday, plant a tree!

HALF BIRTHDAY

This is a great party for a child whose birthday is at an awkward time of the year: it should be held on the six month anniversary of the child's birthday. Party invitations, with the instructions "You Half To Come", can be cut in half. Do everything in halves, like have half a cake with half the candles. Fun activities could include painting half the childrens' faces and stopping games halfway.

KENTUCKY DERBY PARTY

Serve mint iced tea and open-faced party sandwiches. Have your own horse races. Let the guests pick their own horse names, such as Secretariat or Seattle Slew, and then let them race by walking, trotting, cantering, and galloping. Pitch horse shoes. Give ribbons, trophies and small plastic horses as prizes and favors.

NEW YEAR'S EVE

As children arrive, have them make crazy party hats. Hang a large net from the ceiling in the party room and fill with balloons. Decorate calendars for the upcoming year. At the stroke of midnight (or your own designated "midnight"), drop the balloons from the net and serve sparkling cider. Have a Happy New Year parade through the house playing musical instruments from the kitchen, such as pots and pans, and other fun noisemakers.

NUMBER

Use either your child's age or favorite number for lots of numerical fun! Cut large numbers out of construction paper and decorate for invitations. Give favors in sets of the number. Make cookies in the shape of the number and let the guests decorate them. Have number guessing games with objects in small jars that can be given as prizes.

OUTER SPACE

Assign fun names to each child as he or she arrives, such as Mary from Mars. Use these names on planet or star-shaped placecards. Use strings of small holiday lights and balloons decorated as planets to create an out-of-this-world atmosphere. Pack party foods into UFOs, made by attaching two paper plates together with the food inside. Use stickers, glitter, and markers to transform them into flying saucers. Pre-packaged, freeze-dried space foods, sandwiches cut with star-shaped cookie cutters and candy bars with outer space names are the perfect foods.

PIGGIN' OUT

This is a fun outdoor party! Instruct your guests to come dressed in their bathing suits or old clothes and to bring an extra set of clothes. Have all kinds of messy, food related games, such as pie throwing, watermelon seed spitting, egg toss, and gelatin eating contests. Another fun game is to see who can eat a doughnut hanging from a string the fastest. Hose everyone off after all the games are finished and have them change into dry clothes.

RAINBOW

Ask the children to come dressed in their favorite color. Serve rainbow sherbet and other colorful foods. A fun game is the "Rainbow Pass". Wrap a small present in colorful paper. Place another, smaller, present, such as a candy bar, on top and wrap all of it in colored tissue paper. Continue adding layers of the same smaller presents until their total plus the first present equals the total number of children. The children sit in a circle and pass the package while you play music. When the music stops, the child with the package unwraps one layer and keeps what is hidden inside the outer-most layer. Continue starting and stopping the music, making sure each child gets a chance to open a layer, until all the presents are gone.

RUDOLPH PARTY

If your child's birthday falls near Christmas, give him or her a special holiday party everyone will love. As party guests arrive, they can decorate their own personalized stockings with puff paints and then use the stockings as goodie bags. Decorate candy canes to look like Rudolph by using pipe cleaners, little wiggly eyes, and red pompoms and put them into the stockings. Play games like "Musical Sleighs" (musical chairs). Make reindeer faces by tracing each child's foot onto a piece of paper for the face and muzzle and then tracing his or her hands for the antlers. The children can glue on wiggly eyes and a big red nose.

STEP BACK IN TIME

Plan a party for your child's favorite time period. It could be based on medieval, colonial, or pioneer times. Or for more modern fun have a 50's dance or a 70's disco party. Let your imagination run wild to decorate. Guests can come dressed in the appropriate attire for the times.

SUPER HERO-CARTOON

Decorate for this party by using your child's favorite super hero figures or the appropriate stuffed toys to decorate. Party guests can create masks to transform themselves into their favorite super hero or cartoon character. They also might enjoy making their own comic books. Serve foods with fun theme-related names, like Superman sandwiches or Bugs Bunny's All Time Favorite Snack (carrot sticks).

TRAIN

Frost small loaf-sized cakes. Have the children decorate them with candies, cookies and tubes of cake decorating gel. Place the cakes end to end to make a train; round cookies make great wheels. Use your child's toy trains to decorate the party room. Give engineer's hats and whistles as favors. If possible, arrange a trip to a train museum or train specialty shop.

Variations for Games & Activities

Listed here, you will find games and activities from the parties in this book along with ways that you can adapt them to other parties. The suggestions can be used exactly or you and your child can use this list as a guide to creating your own fun activities. When you are planning your party, use some of these ideas to customize your party. This list is also a handy reference if you find you have a lot of extra time to fill in your party, or if the children do not like a certain game.

PLAY CLAY (P.10)

Clay can be formed into many objects fitting any theme: jungle animals, Halloween characters, insects, or water creatures. You may want to provide pictures that can be used for ideas or guides.

DANCING DINOSAURS (P.11)

Children can pretend to be different animals, perhaps moving like a particular creature (slithering like a snake, stalking like a tiger). Elegant ballroom dancing can be done at the Tea Party, clowns can perform at the Under the Big Top Party, or little airplanes can soar and swoop at the Come Fly with Me Party. In addition, the music can be varied to suit the occasion- from classical to a jungle beat.

SCAVENGER HUNT (P.15)

Scavenger Hunts can also be adapted to other themes or subjects. An alphabet hunt can be a fun indoor game in which children locate something from every letter of the alphabet. Children also enjoy hunting for the colors of a rainbow or even for props for the Be A Star Party. A quieter version of the scavenger hunt could involve a search through old magazines for specific objects.

JUNGLE JUMBLE (P.18)

This game is easily varied by assigning different categories of names to the children in the circle: Halloween objects, Christmas decorations, dinosaurs, circus acts, movie stars, or just about anything!

MONKEY TAG (P.18)

Monkey Tag is not limited to an animal theme; simply give it another name. For example, some new names could be "Shark Tag" or "Cowboy Tag". Tag with water guns is fun, too.

ZOODLES (P.19)

Zoodles can be played by assigning words to the players which reflect any theme the party might have. Holiday motifs are one example; objects from nature are another. This game would be appropriate for the Mystery Party in which guessing is involved.

TEDDY BEAR PASS (P.22)

In this game, the teddy bear can be replaced with another stuffed animal, a toy airplane, a ball, or a piece of pirate treasure.

MUSICAL BEARS (P.22)

Musical Bears can be altered for most themes; simply replace the bear shapes with such shapes as fish, dinosaur footprints, airplanes, or cowboy hats.

CLOWN FACES (P.42)

Face painting is a fun activity at many parties. Animal faces are always popular. For the Tea Party or the Be A Star Party, an exaggerated version of glamour make-up could be applied.

PIN THE BADGE ON THE SHERIFF (P.50)

This is a version of the favorite game, "Pin the Tail on the Donkey". With a little creativity you can "Pin the Propeller on the Airplane", "Pin the Patch on the Pirate", "Pin the Smile on the Jack-O-Lantern", "Pin the Bumble Bee on the Flower", or pin the tail on any animal. Just use your imagination!

DRAWING PICTURES WITH YOUR FEET (P.54)

This can be done wherever there is something to draw. Halloween characters, self-portraits, or a version of ZOODLES could even be played with your feet!

CHARADES (P.58)

Charades is also well-suited to various themes. Besides using the party theme itself, you could play by using the children's favorite activities or animals. Party guests could also act out what they want to be when they grow up, or eating their favorite foods.

EASTER HAT RELAY (P.86)

This game can be played with any type of hat, such as cowboy, firefighter or pirate hats. It also could be played with other wearables such as giant shoes for the Under the Big Top Party.

Many of the games in this book could be played at any party. These games include the following:

PUSH-ME-PULL-YOU, P.19

WATER BALLOON TOSS, P.30

EGG IN THE SPOON RACE, P.30

CENTIPEDE RACE, P.30

POTATO RELAY, P.30

BEAN BAG TOSS, P.42

BALLOON SWEEP, P.42

PEANUT PUSH, P.42

POPCORN RACE, P.43

BALLOON POPPING DANCE, P.82

LINKING OF THE PINKIES, P.82

WHO AM I?, P.83

EGG-IN-THE-HAT, P.86

FEATHER-UP, P.86

ORANGE PASS RELAY, P.90

RING TOSS, P.90

BALLOON BRIGADE, P.90

RAINBOW PASS, P.111

AND ANY OF THE GAMES IN THE SPORTS PARTY, PP.46-47

TIPS FOR
CLASSROOM PARTIES

The parties in this book are full of games and activities that are easy to adapt to classroom parties. Many of the recipes are simple to double or triple for large groups and convenient to serve in a classroom.

Some words of advice may help the classroom activities run more smoothly. In any classroom situation, the person in charge is the teacher. He or she is also the best resource that a volunteer planning classroom activities has. Teachers vary in the way they prefer to organize classroom parties. Some teachers plan everything in detail, using volunteers as assistants only. If your child's teacher fits that description, save this section for future classrooms or let the teacher know about this book! Other teachers assign the entire event to the volunteers, but most fall somewhere in between. Whatever crafts or activities you plan, always consult with the teacher beforehand.

When planning an activity, first be sure that it is age-appropriate. The simplest way to test this is to try the idea with your own child. To be absolutely sure that all the students can handle the activity, use a child a year or two younger as a tester, as well. On the other hand, be aware that a project that is too simple will not keep the students' attention.

The activity should also be tested for gender appeal. If all your children are of one gender, it may not be obvious to you which activities will appeal to members of the opposite gender. Consult with the teacher or other parents to be sure.

Collect all materials and equipment in advance. Check with the teacher first. Many teachers have a supply of paper, paints, and scissors, or can obtain them. If other parents are responsible for providing things, do not rely on their children bringing them to school the day of the party!

Have plenty of helpers. The younger the children and the more complicated the activities, the more helpers are needed. If you don't already have a list of other adults who are willing to help, your child's teacher should be able to give you one. Make sure helpers know the directions and rules for the activities beforehand so that class time isn't spent briefing them.

Be aware of the wide variance in the speed with which children create projects. It has nothing to do with ability; children just vary in the amount of attention to detail they prefer. Encourage the helpers to concentrate on the slower workers, but also provide assistance to the speedsters, perhaps by helping them further perfect their creations.

If multiple activities are planned, it is usually more manageable to do them in stations, dividing the class into groups and allowing them a time limit. Be sure to sound a 3 minute warning before the time is up!

Check with the teacher about the school or classroom policy on snacks and treats. Some schools do not permit snacks in the classroom, but allow them to be served to the children at lunchtime. If food is to be served in the morning or close to lunch, vegetables or fruit with dip might be appropriate, or perhaps a breakfast-type of food. The provision of food is a good opportunity for working parents, who cannot come to the classroom during the day, to participate in the occasion.

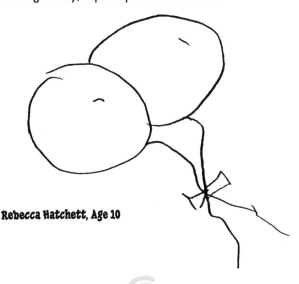

Rebecca Hatchett, Age 10

The following crafts and projects from the parties in this book are easily adaptable to large groups:

PLAY CLAY, P.10

FOSSILS, P.11

BIRD FEEDERS, P.14

FOOD CHAINS, P.14

FLOWER POTS, P.14

BUG EYES, P.14

BIRD BEAK STRAWS, P.15

MARSHMALLOW/GUMDROP ANIMALS, P.17

THUMBPRINT PICTURES, P.18

PAPEL PICADO, P.25

TISSUE PAPER FLOWERS, P.25

NATIVE AMERICAN BRACELETS, P.26

TISSUE PAPER FISH, P.38

FISH PRINTS, P.39 (A bit smelly!)

WESTERN VEST, P.50

GUESSING JAR, P.61

PIRATE HATS & EYE PATCHES, P.66

CHINESE KITES, P.70

ORIGAMI, P.70

ENGLISH CROWNS, P.70

SPANISH CASTINETS, P.71

PARACHUTES, P.74

PATRIOTIC HATS, P.91
(good for Memorial Day, too, since July 4 rarely falls in a school year!)

DRAW THE FACE ON THE PUMPKIN, P.94

PICTURE FRAME MAGNETS, P.99
(can be made in other shapes if school policy so requires)

DECORATING COOKIES, P.102
(this works well for many holidays - Valentine's Day, Halloween, Thanksgiving, St. Patrick's Day - just use the appropriately shaped cookie)

APPLE SANTA FAVORS, P.102

GINGERBREAD HOUSES, P.103
(try to have some time elapse between constructing the houses and decorating them, to let them dry and be more sturdy)

This book is filled with game ideas that can be used for school activities outdoors or in a large space such as a gym. The following games do not involve much movement and can be played in a classroom without a lot of disruption:

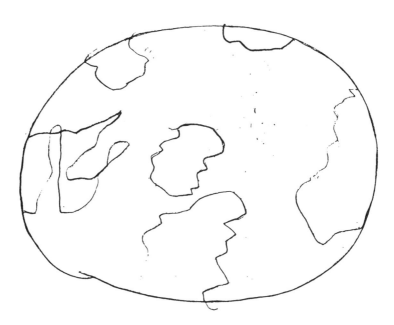

Christie Warthan, Age 8

RECIPES

In this section, you will find recipes from the party menus. The recipes are organized by the party themes. Some items from the menus will not appear here. They are items that can be easily purchased at a grocery store or made at home without a recipe. Feel free to use the menus only as a guideline to developing your own personalized menu with items that are convenient for you and your child.

DINOBURGERS

1 POUND GROUND BEEF
1/4 CUP CHOPPED ONION
1/2 TEASPOON SALT
1/4 TEASPOON GARLIC POWDER
1/2 CUP KETCHUP
1/4 CUP SOUR CREAM
6 HAMBURGER BUNS

In large skillet, cook ground beef and onion until beef is browned. Drain excess fat. Stir in salt, garlic powder, ketchup and sour cream. Simmer for 2 minutes. Serve on hamburger buns. Serves 6.

STEGOSAURUS SALAD

6 LETTUCE LEAVES
12 MARASCHINO CHERRIES, CHOPPED
1 (3 OUNCE) PACKAGE CREAM CHEESE, SOFTENED
6 CANNED PEACH HALVES, DRAINED
12 GRAPES
SLIVERED ALMONDS

Wash lettuce leaves, blot dry and place 1 leaf on each salad plate. Using fork, blend cherries with cream cheese until well mixed. Place a rounded teaspoon of cheese mixture in center of each lettuce leaf and cover with peach half, cut side down. Cut 6 grapes into quarters. Place 4 pieces around each peach half as "feet" and 1 whole grape as "head". Insert slivered almonds in a row across peach for "spikes". Serves 6.

PTERODACTYL EGGS

6 HARD-COOKED EGGS, SHELL REMOVED
1 1/2 TEASPOONS PREPARED MUSTARD
1/4 to 1/3 CUP MAYONNAISE
1 1/2 to 2 TABLESPOONS SWEET PICKLE RELISH
PAPRIKA FOR GARNISH

Cut eggs lengthwise in halves. Carefully remove yolks and set white portion aside. Using fork, mash yolks until smooth. Add mustard, mayonnaise and relish, adjusting amount of mayonnaise to taste. Fill egg white halves with yolk mixture, using spoon or pastry bag with wide tip. Sprinkle with paprika for garnish. Serves 6.

LOCHNESS BARS

1/2 CUP MARGARINE
1 (6 OUNCE) PACKAGE CHOCOLATE CHIPS
1 CUP PEANUT BUTTER
1 (10 1/2 OUNCE) PACKAGE MINIATURE MARSHMALLOWS
4 1/4 CUPS CRISPY RICE CEREAL
1 CUP PEANUTS, OPTIONAL

FROSTING:
1 (6 OUNCE) PACKAGE CHOCOLATE CHIPS
1 (6 OUNCE) PACKAGE BUTTERSCOTCH CHIPS

Combine margarine, chocolate chips and peanut butter in saucepan. Cook over low heat until melted, stirring until smooth. Add marshmallows and stir until melted. Blend in cereal and peanuts. Spread in 13x9x2" baking pan. Chill until firm. Prepare frosting by melting chocolate chips and butterscotch chips together, blending until smooth. Spread on chilled bars. Cut into 2x1" bars. Makes 60.

DINOSAUR CAKE

2 1/4 CUPS ALL-PURPOSE FLOUR
1 TABLESPOON BAKING POWDER
1/2 TEASPOON SALT
3/4 CUP BUTTER OR MARGARINE, SOFTENED
1 1/2 CUPS SUGAR
2 TEASPOONS VANILLA
3 EGGS
1 CUP MILK
ASSORTED CANDIES
PRETZEL STICKS

BUTTERCREAM FROSTING:
1 (16 OUNCE) PACKAGE POWDERED SUGAR
1/2 CUP BUTTER OR MARGARINE, SOFTENED
1 TEASPOON VANILLA
3 TO 4 TABLESPOONS MILK
1/8 TEASPOON SALT
1 1/8 TEASPOONS YELLOW FOOD COLORING

To seal in crumbs before frosting a cake, combine 1 cup apricot or seedless raspberry jam and 1 tablespoon of water and bring to a boil. Allow it to cool, then spread on cake 1 hour before frosting.

DINOSAUR CAKE

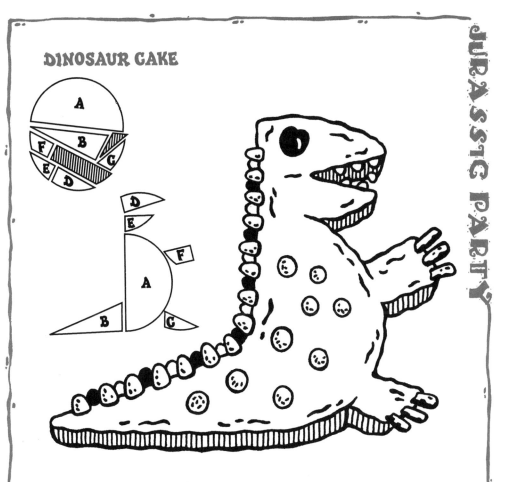

Sift flour, baking powder and salt together. In separate bowl, cream butter and sugar together until smooth. Stir in vanilla. Add eggs, 1 at a time, beating well after each addition. Alternately add dry ingredients and milk, beating well after each addition. Spread batter in 9" springform pan which has been lined with aluminum foil, then greased and floured. Bake at 350 degrees for 45 minutes or until wooden pick inserted at center comes out clean. Cool in pan for 10 minutes. Remove from pan and place on wire rack to complete cooling. Before cutting to form dinosaur shape, freeze cake for 45 minutes. Prepare frosting by blending powdered sugar, butter or margarine, vanilla, milk and salt together until smooth, adding more milk if necessary for good spreading consistency. Stir in food coloring. To shape the dinosaur, cut cake according to diagram. Arrange on 16x16" foil-covered cardboard. Use frosting to hold pieces together. Spread frosting on top and sides of assembled dinosaur. Decorate with candy such as gumdrops, jelly beans and candy corn. Use pretzel sticks for teeth and claws. Serves 10.

T. REX PUNCH

1 (6 OUNCE) CAN FROZEN LEMONADE CONCENTRATE, THAWED
1 (6 OUNCE) CAN FROZEN LIMEADE CONCENTRATE, THAWED
6 (6 OUNCE) CANS WATER
1/2 (46 OUNCE) CAN GRAPEFRUIT JUICE
1/2 (46 OUNCE) CAN PINEAPPLE JUICE
1/2 TO 1 CUP SUGAR (TO TASTE)
GREEN FOOD COLORING
1 (32 OUNCE) BOTTLE GINGER ALE

Combine lemonade and limeade concentrates, water, grapefruit and pineapple juices, sugar and green food coloring. Pour into round plastic containers and freeze. To serve, partially thaw punch, break into chunks and place in punch bowl. Add ginger ale just before serving. Serves 20.

. . . .

PLAY CLAY
NON-EDIBLE

1/4 CUP VEGETABLE OIL
2 CUPS WATER
2 CUPS ALL-PURPOSE FLOUR
1 CUP SALT
1 (2 1/2 OUNCE) CAN CREAM OF TARTAR
FOOD COLORIING

Pour oil and water into large saucepan. Add flour, salt and cream of tartar; blending thoroughly. Cook over medium heat, stirring constantly, until very thick. Remove from heat and let stand until cool. To color clay, knead food coloring, a few drops at a time, into portions of dough.

. . . .

PIGS IN A BLANKET

1 (8 OUNCE) CAN REFRIGERATED DINNER ROLLS
8 HOT DOGS
8 (3x1/2x1/4") STRIPS CHEDDAR CHEESE

Separate dough into 8 pieces. Cut slit in each hot dog and place cheese in slit. Shape 1 piece of dough around each hot dog, pinching edges to seal. Place on lightly-greased baking sheet. Bake at 400 degrees for 15 to 20 minutes or until browned. Serve with ketchup and mustard. Serves 8.

TRAIL MIX

PEANUTS
MINIATURE MARSHMALLOWS
RAISINS
SUNFLOWER SEEDS, SHELLED
O-SHAPED OAT CEREAL
CANDY COATED CHOCOLATE PIECES

Combine peanuts, marshmallows, raisins, sunflower seeds, cereal and candy in proportions to suit children's tastes.

CHOCOLATE FONDUE WITH FRUIT

4 (1 OUNCE) SQUARES SEMI-SWEET CHOCOLATE
1 CUP HALF AND HALF CREAM
1 CUP SUGAR
1/2 TEASPOON VANILLA
ASSORTED FRUIT

Place chocolate and half and half in microwave-safe 1-quart casserole. Microwave at medium setting (50%) for 5 to 6 minutes or until chocolate is melted. Stir well. Add sugar and vanilla. Microwave at medium for 3 to 4 minutes or until sugar is dissolved. Serve immediately from casserole or transfer to fondue pot. Serve with fruit such as apple and pear wedges, banana and pineapple chunks, strawberries or cherries. Makes 2 cups.

DIRT CUPS WITH GUMMIE WORMS

1 (16 OUNCE) PACKAGE CHOCOLATE SANDWICH COOKIES
2 CUPS MILK
1 (3 3/4 OUNCE) PACKAGE CHOCOLATE INSTANT PUDDING MIX
1 (8 OUNCE) CARTON FROZEN WHIPPED TOPPING, THAWED
CANDY GUMMIE WORMS
CHOCOLATE COVERED RAISINS (OPTIONAL)

Crush cookies in food processor or place in zipper-lock plastic bag and crush with rolling pin. Set crumbs aside. Combine milk and pudding mix. Using wire whisk, beat for 2 minutes. Let stand for 5 minutes. Fold in whipped topping and 1/2 of cookie crumbs. Place 1 tablespoon reserved crumbs in each of 8 (7 ounce) paper or plastic cups. Spoon pudding into each cup, filling about 3/4 full. Top with remaining crumbs. Chill for 1 hour or until ready to serve. Place gummie worms on crumb topping and gently push below surface. Add a few covered raisins as "rocks" on top of crumb "dirt". Serves 8.

LADYBUG CAKE

1 (18 1/2 OUNCE) PACKAGE CAKE MIX
1 (16 OUNCE) CAN WHITE FROSTING
BLACK AND RED GUM DROPS
BLACK AND RED SHOESTRING LICORICE
RED DECORATOR SUGAR

Prepare cake mix according to package directions. Pour batter into greased and floured 1 1/2-quart oven-proof bowl (glass or metal). Bake at 350 degrees for 1 hour and 5 to 10 minutes or until wooden pick inserted near center comes out clean. Cooking time will vary depending on type of dish or pan used. Cool cake for 10 minutes, then remove and place on wire rack to complete cooling. Place cooled cake, flat side down, on serving plate. Spread frosting on cake, covering smoothly. Arrange "face" features on one side: use black gumdrop slices for eyes, red gumdrop slice for nose, red licorice for mouth and black licorice for eyebrows and antennae. Leaving a space of about 2" from curved edge of "face", sprinkle red sugar on remainder of cake. Place black gumdrop slices for spots and black licorice for a stripe across the center of the shell. Serves 8.

RAINBOW FLOATS

1 QUART RAINBOW SHERBET
1 (32 OUNCE) BOTTLE GINGER ALE, CHILLED

Place scoop of sherbet in each of 8 glasses. Add ginger ale; carbonation will make the sherbet frothy so do not fill to rim. Serves 8.

SNAKE SANDWICH

1 LARGE LOAF FRENCH BREAD
8 SLICES HAM OR OTHER LUNCHEON MEAT
8 SLICES AMERICAN CHEESE
MAYONNAISE
2 CARROT STICKS
2 BLACK OLIVES
RED BELL PEPPER STRIPS

Cut loaf in 10 slices. Place on oblong serving tray. Make 8 sandwiches, inserting ham and cheese between bread slices and spreading with mayonnaise; reserve end slices of loaf. Use 1 end slice to make snake's head: cut piece horizontally for mouth, insert carrot sticks for fangs and a red pepper strip for tongue, add two triangle shapes of red pepper for nostrils and press olives into bread for eyes. Decorate remaining end piece of bread with red pepper strips for rattles or stripes. Serves 8.

MONKEY BREAD

3 (8 OUNCE) CANS REFRIGERATED BISCUIT DOUGH
1 CUP SUGAR
1 TEASPOON CINNAMON
1/2 CUP BUTTER
1 CUP FIRMLY-PACKED BROWN SUGAR

Separate biscuit dough pieces and cut each in 4 sections. Combine white sugar and cinnamon. Pour into brown paper bag, add biscuit pieces, a handful at a time, and shake to coat well. Layer pieces in greased and floured 10" tube pan. Melt butter. Blend in brown sugar and pour mixture over biscuit pieces. Bake at 350 degrees for 20 minutes. Serves 12.

TROPICAL FRUIT TRAY

BANANAS
KIWI FRUIT
ORANGE JUICE
MANDARIN ORANGE SECTIONS
SEEDLESS GRAPES

Peel and cut bananas and kiwi in bite-sized slices, brushing with small amount of orange juice to avoid discoloration. (Children prefer flavor of orange juice to lemon juice.) Arrange with orange sections and grapes on tray or platter.

. . . .

PEANUTTY MONKEY BARS

1/3 CUP SUGAR
1/2 CUP PEANUT BUTTER
1 (8 OUNCE) PACKAGE CREAM CHEESE, SOFTENED
2 EGGS
1 (18 1/2 OUNCE) PACKAGE BANANA CAKE MIX
1 1/4 CUPS QUICK-COOKING ROLLED OATS, DIVIDED
1/2 CUP MARGARINE OR BUTTER, SOFTENED, DIVIDED
1/2 CUP CHOPPED PEANUTS
1/4 CUP FIRMLY-PACKED BROWN SUGAR

Blend sugar, peanut butter, cream cheese and 1 egg together until smooth. Set aside. Combine cake mix, 1 cup oats and 6 tablespoons margarine or butter. Mix until crumbly. Reserving 1 cup crumbs for topping, add 1 egg to remaining crumbs and mix until well blended. Press in bottom of greased and floured 13x9x2" baking pan. Pour cream cheese filling over crust, spreading to cover. Combine reserved crumbs, 1/4 cup oats, 2 tablespoons margarine, peanuts and brown sugar, mixing well. Sprinkle crumb mixture evenly over filling. Bake at 350 degrees for 25 to 35 minutes or until golden brown. Cool before cutting into 3x1" bars. Makes 36.

LION CAKE

1 (18 1/2 OUNCE) PACKAGE CHOCOLATE CAKE MIX
VANILLA WAFERS
GUMDROPS
SHOESTRING LICORICE

PEANUT BUTTER FROSTING:
4 1/2 CUPS POWDERED SUGAR
1/2 CUP PEANUT BUTTER
1/3 TO 1/2 CUP SKIM MILK

Make your cake ahead of time and freeze well-wrapped. Before the party, frost it while still frozen. Fewer crumbs will get in the frosting.

Prepare cake mix according to package instructions, baking in 2 round 9" baking pans. Cool in pans for 10 minutes, then remove and place on wire rack to complete cooling. Prepare frosting by blending powdered sugar, peanut butter and milk together until smooth. Place 1 cake layer on serving plate, spread with frosting, top with second layer and frost top and sides of assembled cake. Arrange vanilla wafers around edge of top of cake, overlapping slightly for the mane. Place gum drop slices on cake for eyes and nose and licorice for the mouth and whiskers. Serves 12.

JUNGLE PUNCH

1 QUART ORANGE OR LEMON SHERBET
1/2 CUP FROZEN ORANGE JUICE CONCENTRATE
1 1/2 CUPS COLD WATER
2 (12 OUNCE) CANS GINGER ALE, CHILLED

Combine sherbet, orange juice concentrate and cold water in blender container. Blend until smooth. Add ginger ale and stir gently. Serve immediately. Makes 8 cups.

HONEY BEE AMBROSIA

4 MEDIUM ORANGES
3 BANANAS
1/2 CUP ORANGE JUICE
1/4 CUP HONEY
2 TABLESPOONS LEMON JUICE
1/4 CUP FLAKED COCONUT
MARASCHINO CHERRY HALVES (OPTIONAL)

Peel fruit; separate oranges into sections and slice bananas. Combine orange juice, honey and lemon juice. Pour over fruit and mix well. Sprinkle with coconut. Chill, covered, for at least 1 hour. Garnish with maraschino cherries. Serves 6.

. . . .

BIG BEAR SUNDAES

CHOCOLATE ICE CREAM
ROUND COOKIES
SMALL CANDIES

Place a scoop of ice cream on small individual serving plate. Insert 2 cookies in each ice cream ball to form ears. Use small candies for eyes and nose. Freeze until ready to serve.

. . . .

TEDDY BEAR CAKE

1 (18 1/2 OUNCE) PACKAGE CAKE MIX
BUTTER CREAM FROSTING (PAGE 120)
FLAKED COCONUT
ROUND COOKIES
GUM DROPS
SHOESTRING LICORICE

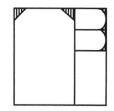

Prepare cake mix according to package directions. Pour slightly more than 1/2 of batter into greased and floured 9x9x2" cake pan, use remainder to make cupcakes and bake as directed. Cool cake in pan for 10 minutes, then remove to wire rack to complete cooling. Cut cake according to diagram. Assemble, using frosting to hold pieces together. Spread frosting on top and sides of cake. Lightly press coconut onto frosting for "fur". Arrange cookies and gum drop slices for eyes and nose and licorice for mouth. White sprinkles or shaved white chocolate can be substituted for coconut. Spread remaining frosting on cupcakes and set aside for dessert or snack next day. Serves 8.

HONEY BALLS

1/2 CUP HONEY
1/2 CUP PEANUT BUTTER
2 CUPS CRUSHED VANILLA WAFERS
1/2 CUP POWDERED SUGAR

Combine honey and peanut butter, mixing until smooth. Stir in wafer crumbs. Shape into small balls and roll in powdered sugar. Makes 2-3 dozen.

TACOS

1 POUND LEAN GROUND BEEF
1/2 CUP WATER
8 TACO SHELLS

SEASONING:
2 TEASPOONS INSTANT MINCED ONION
1 TEASPOON SALT
1 TEASPOON CHILI POWDER
1/2 TEASPOON CORNSTARCH
1/2 TEASPOON GROUND CUMIN
1/2 TEASPOON INSTANT MINCED GARLIC
1/4 TEASPOON DRIED OREGANO

In skillet over medium-high heat, cook ground beef until browned, stirring to crumble. While beef cooks, prepare seasoning by mixing onion, salt, chili powder, cornstarch, cumin, garlic and oregano. Or substitute a packet of prepared taco seasoning. Drain excess fat from beef. Stir in water and seasoning. Reduce heat and simmer for 10 minutes, stirring occasionally. Warm taco shells according to package directions. Spoon meat filling into each. Serves 8.

CURLY TACO MIX

1/4 CUP BUTTER OR MARGARINE
1 TEASPOON CHILI POWDER
1/2 TEASPOON GROUND CUMIN
3 CUPS SMALL CORN CHIPS
2 CUPS PUFFED CHEESE CURLS
1 CUP SHELLED PUMPKIN SEEDS OR PEANUTS (OPTIONAL)

Place butter or margarine in 13x9x2" baking pan. Bake at 300 degrees for 3 to 5 minutes or until butter is melted. Stir in chili powder and cumin. Add corn chips, cheese curls and pumpkin seeds or peanuts, stirring to mix thoroughly. Bake at 300 degrees for 15 minutes, stirring once or twice. Cool, then store in tightly-covered container. For microwave preparation, melt butter or margarine in microwave-safe bowl at high setting (100%) for about 1 minute. Stir in chili powder, cumin, chips, cheese curls and seeds or peanuts, mixing well. Microwave on high setting for 6 minutes, stirring every 2 minutes. Makes 5 cups.

SOUTHWESTERN LAYERED DIP

2 (10 1/2 OUNCE) CANS JALAPENO BEAN DIP
3 RIPE MEDIUM AVOCADOS
JUICE OF 1 LEMON
SALT AND BLACK PEPPER TO TASTE
1 CUP SOUR CREAM
1/2 CUP MAYONNAISE
1 PACKET TACO SEASONING MIX
1/2 CUP CHOPPED GREEN ONION

2 MEDIUM TOMATOES, PEELED, CHOPPED AND DRAINED
1 (6 OUNCE) CAN PITTED BLACK OLIVES, DRAINED AND SLICED
3 CUPS (12 OUNCES) GRATED SHARP CHEDDAR CHEESE
CORN CHIPS

On large round or oval plate, layer ingredients in following order: bean dip, avocados mashed and mixed with lemon juice and seasoned with salt and black pepper, sour cream mixed with mayonnaise and taco seasoning, onion, tomatoes, olives and cheese. Chill for a few hours to blend flavors. Serve with corn chips. Makes about 8 cups.

GIANT COOKIE

1/4 CUP SUGAR
1/3 CUP FIRMLY-PACKED BROWN SUGAR
1/2 CUP VEGETABLE SHORTENING
1/2 TEASPOON VANILLA
1 EGG
1 1/4 CUPS ALL-PURPOSE FLOUR

1/2 TEASPOON BAKING SODA
1/4 TEASPOON SALT
1 (6 OUNCE) PACKAGE SEMI-SWEET CHOCOLATE CHIPS
1/2 CUP CHOPPED NUTS
1 TUBE DECORATOR FROSTING OR DECORATING GEL

Cream sugar, brown sugar and shortening together until light and fluffy. Add vanilla and egg, blending thoroughly. Combine flour, baking soda and salt. Add to creamed ingredients and mix well. Stir in chocolate chips and nuts. Place dough on baking sheet or pizza pan which has been covered with aluminum foil, then greased. With floured fingers, spread dough to form 12-inch circle. Bake at 350 degrees for 17 to 21 minutes or until slightly firm when touched in center. Cool completely before removing from foil. Place on serving tray. With frosting or gel, decorate with southwestern motifs such as setting sun or cactus. Cut in wedges or squares to serve. Makes 24 to 30.

INNOCENT MARGARITAS

1 (12 OUNCE) CAN FROZEN LEMONADE CONCENTRATE
1 (12 OUNCE) CAN FROZEN LIMEADE CONCENTRATE
1 (12 OUNCE) CAN LEMON-LIME CARBONATED DRINK
ICE

Using 1/2 of each ingredient, combine lemonade and limeade concentrates and carbonated drink in blender container. Blend until smooth. Add ice and blend until slushy and smooth. Repeat with remaining ingredients. Serves 8.

OVEN FRIED CHICKEN

6 BONELESS CHICKEN BREAST HALVES (SKIN ON OR SKINLESS)
1 CUP ALL-PURPOSE FLOUR
2 TEASPOONS SALT
1/2 TEASPOON BLACK PEPPER
1/2 TEASPOON PAPRIKA
1/2 CUP MARGARINE

Place chicken pieces in paper bag with flour, salt, black pepper and paprika. Shake to coat well. Place margarine in 13x9x2" baking dish lined with aluminum foil. Bake at 400 degrees until margarine sizzles. Place chicken, skin side down, in dish. Bake for 30 minutes, turn pieces and bake for additional 30 minutes; do not cover. Serves 6.

BAKED BEANS

2 (16 OUNCE) CANS BAKED BEANS
2 TABLESPOONS FIRMLY-PACKED BROWN SUGAR
1 TABLESPOON MOLASSES
1 TEASPOON CINNAMON

Combine beans, brown sugar, molasses and cinnamon in saucepan. Simmer for 15 to 20 minutes until thoroughly heated. Serves 6.

SUNDAE SAUCES
QUICK CHOCOLATE SAUCE

1 CUP SUGAR
1/3 CUP COCOA
2 TABLESPOONS ALL-PURPOSE FLOUR
1/4 TEASPOON SALT
1 TABLESPOON BUTTER
1 CUP BOILING WATER
1 TEASPOON VANILLA

Combine sugar, cocoa, flour, salt and butter in microwave-safe bowl, mixing well. Gradually blend in water. Microwave, covered, at high setting (100%) for about 3 minutes or until smooth and thickened. Stir in vanilla. Makes 1 3/4 cups.

HOT FUDGE SAUCE

1 (1 OUNCE) SQUARE UNSWEETENED CHOCOLATE
1 (14 OUNCE) CAN SWEETENED CONDENSED MILK

Melt chocolate in small saucepan over very low heat. Remove from heat and blend in milk. Makes 1 1/3 cups.

PECAN PRALINE SAUCE

1/2 CUP LIGHT CORN SYRUP
1/3 CUP FIRMLY-PACKED LIGHT BROWN SUGAR
3 TABLESPOONS BUTTER
1/8 TEASPOON SALT
2 TABLESPOONS EVAPORATED MILK
1/2 CUP FINELY CHOPPED PECANS

Combine syrup, brown sugar, butter and salt in microwave-safe bowl. Microwave at high setting (100%) for 2 1/2 to 3 minutes or until thick and bubbly; do not overcook. Cool for 5 minutes. Stir in milk and pecans. Chill until ready to use. Makes 1 1/4 cups.

BUTTERSCOTCH SAUCE

1 CUP FIRMLY-PACKED BROWN SUGAR
2 TABLESPOONS ALL-PURPOSE FLOUR
1/4 CUP EVAPORATED MILK
1/4 CUP BUTTER, MELTED

Combine brown sugar and flour in microwave-safe bowl. Blend in milk and butter. Microwave at high setting (100%) for 2 to 4 minutes or until bubbly; stir well and microwave for additional 3 minutes. Serve warm. Makes 1 1/2 cups.

VEGGIE TRAY AND DIP

CARROT STICKS
CELERY STICKS
CUCUMBER OR ZUCCHINI SLICES
BROCCOLI FLOWERETS
SMALL HEAD RED CABBAGE
BLUE CHEESE OR RANCH SALAD DRESSING

Arrange vegetables in ring on serving tray. Core cabbage and hollow out to form a "bowl". Spoon salad dressing into cabbage "bowl". Place in center of vegetables.

. . . .

SCONES

13/4 CUPS ALL-PURPOSE FLOUR
1 TABLESPOON SUGAR
2 1/2 TEASPOONS BAKING POWDER
1/2 TEASPOON SALT
1/4 CUP PLUS 2 TABLESPOONS MARGARINE
2 EGGS
1/3 CUP MILK
SUGAR

Combine flour, 1 tablespoon sugar, baking powder and salt. Cut in margarine until mixture forms coarse crumbs. Beat eggs. Reserving 1 tablespoon egg liquid, add milk to remainder. Stir egg-milk mixture into dry ingredients and mix well. Place dough on lightly-floured surface and roll to 1/2-inch thickness. Cut into 3x3" squares, then cut diagonally to form 2 triangles from each piece. Place 1" apart on greased baking sheet. Brush with reserved egg and sprinkle with sugar. Bake at 425 degrees for 10 to 25 minutes or until golden. Serve with butter and jam. Serves 10 to 12.

PETIT FOURS

1/2 CUP PLUS 1 TABLESPOON MARGARINE, SOFTENED
11/4 CUPS SUGAR
3 EGGS
2 CUPS ALL-PURPOSE FLOUR
1 TABLESPOON BAKING POWDER
1/2 TEASPOON SALT
3/4 CUP MILK
STRAWBERRY JAM

SUGAR SYRUP:
1 CUP SUGAR
1 CUP WATER

FROSTING:
6 CUPS SIFTED POWDERED SUGAR
1/4 CUP PLUS 1 TABLESPOON WATER
1/4 CUP PLUS 1 TABLESPOON LIGHT CORN SYRUP
1 TEASPOON VANILLA
FOOD COLORING

Cream margarine and sugar together until smooth. Add eggs, 1 at a time, beating well after each addition. Combine flour, baking powder and salt. Alternately add dry ingredients and milk to creamed mixture. Spread batter in greased 13x9x2" baking pan. Bake at 375 degrees for 25 to 30 minutes. Cool in pan for 10 minutes, then remove to wire rack to complete cooling. Wrap cake tightly in aluminum foil and freeze for several hours or until firm. For syrup, combine sugar and water in saucepan. Bring to a boil, reduce heat and simmer for 10 minutes. For frosting, combine powdered sugar, water, corn syrup and vanilla in top of double boiler. Over boiling water, cook until sugar is melted and frosting is smooth and glossy. Tint with food coloring. To assemble Petit Fours, cut frozen cake horizontally. Brush sugar syrup on both layers. Spread jam on lower layer and replace with top layer. Cut into 2x2" squares. Place squares apart on wire rack over shallow pan. Pour warm frosting over squares, completely covering top and sides and reusing excess frosting from shallow pan (reheating and adding small amount of water if necessary for consistency); cover all cakes. Let stand until dry. Makes 24.

TUNA SAILS

1 (3 1/4 OUNCE) CAN TUNA, DRAINED AND FLAKED
1/4 CUP MAYONNAISE OR SALAD DRESSING
1/4 CUP CHOPPED APPLE
2 TABLESPOONS SUNFLOWER SEEDS, SHELLED
2 WHOLE GRAIN ENGLISH MUFFINS
8 TRIANGULAR TORTILLA CHIPS

Combine tuna, mayonnaise or salad dressing, apple and sunflower seeds, mixing well. Split and toast muffins. On each muffin half, spread 1/4 of tuna mixture. For sails, insert 2 chips, short side down, into tuna mixture on each muffin. Serves 4.

SKEWERED FRUIT

APPLE CHUNKS
FRESH PINEAPPLE CHUNKS
BANANA CHUNKS
WHOLE STRAWBERRIES
MELON BALLS
ORANGE JUICE

Toss fresh fruit chunks or pieces with small amount of orange juice (to prevent discoloration). Place fruit on wooden skewers to serve.

GELATIN FISHBOWL

3 (3 OUNCE) PACKAGES BLUE COLORED GELATIN
VANILLA WAFERS, CRUSHED
GUMMIE FISH AND SHELLS

Prepare gelatin according to package directions. Chill until partially thickened. In fish bowl, line bottom with wafer crumbs. Spoon in gelatin, adding gummie fish and shells to resemble aquarium. Chill until firm. Use fishbowl as centerpiece for table, then serve. Serves 8 to 12.

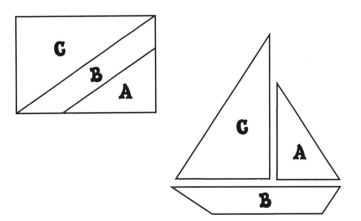

SAILBOAT CAKE

1 (18 1/2 OUNCE) PACKAGE WHITE OR YELLOW CAKE MIX

WHITE FROSTING:
1 CUP VEGETABLE SHORTENING
1/2 TEASPOON ALMOND EXTRACT
6 CUPS SIFTED POWDERED SUGAR
1/4 TO 1/3 CUP MILK
FOOD COLORING

Prepare cake according to package directions. Bake in 13x9x2" baking pan. Cool in pan for 10 minutes, then remove to wire rack to complete cooling. Prepare frosting by combining shortening and almond extract. Beat with electric mixer at medium speed for 30 seconds. Gradually add 1/2 of powdered sugar, beating well. Add 1/4 cup milk. Gradually add remaining powdered sugar and enough of remaining milk to form spreading consistency. Cut cake according to diagram. Arrange in sailboat shape on serving tray or foil-covered cardboard. Tint portion of frosting for boat section and frost. Spread white frosting on sails. Serves 12 to 16.

FROTHY SEAS

1 (6 OUNCE) CAN FROZEN GRAPE JUICE CONCENTRATE
1 CUP MILK
2 CUPS VANILLA ICE CREAM

Combine grape juice concentrate, milk and ice cream in blender container. Blend for 30 seconds. Pour into cups and add paper umbrellas. Serves 6 to 8.

CARAMEL APPLES

6 MEDIUM APPLES
6 ICE CREAM STICKS
1 (14 OUNCE) PACKAGE CARAMELS
3 TABLESPOONS WATER
1/4 CUP CREAMY PEANUT BUTTER
1/2 TEASPOON CINNAMON
1/4 CUP PLUS 2 TABLESPOONS CHOPPED SALTED PEANUTS

Insert ice cream sticks in stem ends of apples. Combine caramels, water, peanut butter and cinnamon in top of double boiler. Cook over boiling water until caramels are melted and mixture is smooth, stirring frequently. Dip each apple in caramel coating, then roll in chopped peanuts. Chill for about 1 hour or until coating is firm. Serves 6.

POPCORN CLUSTERS

3/4 CUP UNPOPPED POPCORN
1 TO 2 CUPS PEANUTS
1 CUP MARGARINE
2 CUPS FIRMLY-PACKED BROWN SUGAR
1/2 CUP LIGHT CORN SYRUP
1/2 TEASPOON SALT
1 TEASPOON VANILLA
1/2 TEASPOON BAKING SODA

Use caution when serving popcorn or nuts as they may be a choking hazard to young children.

Pop corn. Place with peanuts in large baking or roasting pan. Combine margarine, brown sugar, syrup, salt and vanilla in saucepan. Bring to a boil and cook for 5 minutes; do not overcook. Remove from heat and stir in baking soda. Pour mixture over popcorn and peanuts. Stir until coated. Bake at 250 degrees for 2 hours, stirring occasionally. Store in air-tight container.

SNOWCONES

5 CUPS SHAVED ICE
1 (6 OUNCE) CAN FROZEN GRAPE JUICE CONCENTRATE, THAWED

Using an ice cream scoop, place 2 scoops ice in plastic cones or dishes. Spoon 2 tablespoons undiluted grape juice concentrate over each cone. Serve with straws or spoons. Serves 6.

CLOWNFACE ICE CREAM

1 QUART VANILLA ICE CREAM
CANDY COATED CHOCOLATE CANDIES
FLAKED COCONUT
SUGAR ICE CREAM CONES
CHERRIES

To color flaked coconut, place it in a recloseable bag along with a few drops of food coloring and shake well.

Place single scoops of ice cream in cupcake liners on baking sheet. Press candies into each scoop for eyes and nose and add flaked coconut for hair. Top with sugar cone hat decorated with cherry "pompom". Freeze until ready to serve. Serves 6 to 8.

ICE CREAM CONE CUPCAKES

1 (18 1/2 OUNCE) PACKAGE CHOCOLATE, YELLOW OR WHITE CAKE MIX
FLAT-BOTTOM WAFER ICE CREAM CONES
BUTTER CREAM FROSTING (PAGE 120)
SPRINKLES

Prepare cake mix according to package directions. Spoon batter into cones set in muffin pans, filling 3/4 full. Bake according to package directions for cupcakes. Cool, then mound frosting on cake portion and decorate with sprinkles. Makes 18 to 24.

POLKA DOT PUNCH

2 (12 OUNCE) CANS LEMON-LIME CARBONATED SOFT DRINK
1 (46 OUNCE) CAN PUNCH DRINK

Pour soft drink into ice cube trays. Freeze. Serve punch with ice cubes. Serves 6 to 8.

FAVORITE BALL CAKE

Follow directions for baking LADYBUG CAKE (PAGE 124).
To decorate cake as a baseball or soccer ball, spread with
white frosting. Trim with red or blue tinted frosting, according
to diagrams. To decorate as a basketball, tint the frosting
orange and trim with brown frosting.

Make well-
rounded scoops of
ice cream ahead of
time to serve
quickly with cake.
Place them in
paper baking cups,
top with colored
decorator sugar,
and store in
freezer on a
cookie sheet until
serving time.

COLESLAW

1 MEDIUM HEAD CABBAGE
1/4 CUP SUGAR
1/4 CUP VINEGAR
1/2 CUP MAYONNAISE
1 TEASPOON SALT
1/2 TEASPOON BLACK PEPPER

Shred cabbage. Combine sugar, vinegar, mayonnaise, salt and black pepper. Add to cabbage and mix well. Chill for 1/2 to 1 hour before serving. Serves 6 to 8.

COWBOY COOKIES

2 CUPS ALL-PURPOSE FLOUR
1/2 TEASPOON BAKING POWDER
2 TEASPOONS BAKING SODA
1/2 TEASPOON SALT
1 CUP SUGAR
1 CUP FIRMLY-PACKED BROWN SUGAR
3/4 CUP VEGETABLE SHORTENING
2 EGGS
2 CUPS UNCOOKED ROLLED OATS
1/2 TEASPOON VANILLA
1 (6 OUNCE) PACKAGE CHOCOLATE CHIPS

Sift flour, baking powder, baking soda and salt together. Cream sugar, brown sugar and shortening together until smooth. Add eggs and beat until fluffy. Add dry ingredients to creamed mixture and mix well. Stir in oats, vanilla and chocolate chips. Dough will be crumbly. Drop by teaspoonfuls on greased baking sheet. Bake at 350 degrees for 15 minutes. Makes 36 to 48.

SHERIFF'S BADGE CAKE

1 (18 1/2 OUNCE) PACKAGE CHOCOLATE, WHITE OR YELLOW CAKE MIX
BUTTER CREAM FROSTING (PAGE 120) OR FAVORITE FROSTING
1 TUBE PREPARED DECORATOR FROSTING

Prepare cake according to package directions. Bake in 2 round 8" or 9" baking pans. Cool in pans for 10 minutes, then remove to wire rack to complete cooling. Frost top of 1 layer, add remaining layer and spread frosting smoothly on sides and top of cake. For badge design, draw 2 equilateral triangles, 6" on each side. Cut out and place 1 overlapping the other, upside down, to form 6-pointed star. Trace shape onto wax paper and cut out. Gently place pattern on top of cake and trace outline with wooden pick. Remove wax paper. Following the lines, define the badge shape with contrasting color frosting from the tube. Make large dots at the points of the star and write "SHERIFF" and child's name within the star shape. Serves 10 to 12.

BRANDED PANCAKES

1 1/4 CUPS SIFTED ALL-PURPOSE FLOUR
1 TABLESPOON SUGAR
1 TABLESPOON BAKING POWDER
1/2 TEASPOON SALT
1 EGG, BEATEN
1 CUP MILK
2 TABLESPOONS VEGETABLE OIL

Sift flour, sugar, baking powder and salt together. Combine egg, milk and oil. Add liquid to dry ingredients and stir just until moistened. Drizzle batter in mirror image of desired "brand" initial on hot griddle and cook, turning once. For thinner pancakes, increase milk by 2 tablespoons. Serves 4 to 6.

SPAGHETTI

1 POUND GROUND BEEF
1 ONION, CHOPPED
2 CLOVES GARLIC, MINCED
3 (8 OUNCE) CANS TOMATO SAUCE
1 CUP RED WINE
1 TABLESPOON SUGAR
1 TEASPOON ITALIAN SEASONING
BLACK PEPPER TO TASTE
2 CUPS (16 OUNCES) BROKEN VERMICELLI
2 CUPS (8 OUNCES) GRATED CHEDDAR CHEESE
GRATED PARMESAN CHEESE

In skillet, brown beef, stirring to crumble. Add onion and garlic and cook until tender. Drain excess fat. Stir in tomato sauce, wine, sugar, seasoning and black pepper. Simmer for 30 minutes. Prepare vermicelli according to package directions, cooking just until al dente. Drain well. Combine sauce, vermicelli and 1/2 cup Cheddar cheese. Spread mixture in greased 13x9x2" baking dish. Sprinkle with remaining Cheddar cheese and top with Parmesan cheese. Bake, covered with aluminum foil, at 325 degrees for 45 minutes; remove foil and continue baking for 15 minutes. Serves 6.

. . . .

PANCAKES

Prepare batter as instructed for BRANDED PANCAKES (page 142). Spoon batter onto hot griddle and cook, turning once. Serves 6.

Pancakes are easy to make ahead of time and freeze. Just reheat in the microwave and serve!

CHICKEN KABOBS

1 TABLESPOON CHOPPED PARSLEY
1/2 TEASPOON BASIL
1/2 TEASPOON OREGANO
1/2 CUP VEGETABLE OIL
1/4 CUP WHITE WINE VINEGAR
1 TABLESPOON WORCESTERSHIRE SAUCE
1 1/2 POUNDS CHICKEN BREAST, SKIN AND BONE REMOVED
4 EARS CORN
1 LARGE OR 2 MEDIUM RED BELL PEPPERS

Combine parsley, basil, oregano, oil, vinegar and Worcestershire sauce in small jar with tight-fitting lid. Shake until well blended. Set aside. Cut chicken into 24 pieces, corn into 12 pieces and bell pepper into 12 pieces. On each of 6 metal 10-inch skewers, alternately thread 4 pieces chicken, 2 pieces corn and 2 pieces bell pepper. Place in 13x9x2" baking dish. Brush all sides of chicken and vegetables with marinade. Chill, covered, for 45 minutes. Prepare grill. Place kabobs on grill about 8 inches from medium coals. Cook for 10 to 15 minutes or until chicken is no longer pink and vegetables are crisp-tender, turning and brushing frequently with marinade. For broiler method, broil kabobs 4 to 6 inches from heat source for 14 to 18 minutes or until done, turning once and brushing with marinade. Serves 6.

. . . .

FRUIT BOWL

APPLE WEDGES
BANANA CHUNKS
WHOLE GRAPES
ORANGE SECTIONS
ORANGE JUICE
SUGAR

Combine apple, bananas, grapes and oranges. Toss with small amount of orange juice to prevent discoloration and sweeten to taste with sugar.

CHILI

2 POUNDS COARSELY GROUND CHUCK
2 (15 OUNCE) CANS RED KIDNEY BEANS
2 (14 1/2 OUNCE) CANS CRUSHED OR STEWED TOMATOES
2 MEDIUM-SIZED ONIONS, COARSELY CHOPPED
1 LARGE GREEN BELL PEPPER, COARSELY CHOPPED
2 CLOVES GARLIC, CRUSHED
2 TO 3 TABLESPOONS CHILI POWDER
1 TEASPOON BLACK PEPPER
1 TEASPOON GROUND CUMIN
SALT TO TASTE

In large skillet, cook beef until browned. Drain excess fat. Combine beef, beans, tomatoes, onion, bell pepper, garlic, chili powder, black pepper, cumin and salt in large saucepan. Simmer, covered, for 1 1/2 to 2 hours. Or combine all ingredients in slow cooker and cook, covered, at low setting for 10 to 12 hours or at high setting for 5 to 6 hours. Serves 8.

CORN MUFFINS

1 CUP CORNMEAL
1 CUP ALL-PURPOSE FLOUR
1 TABLESPOON SUGAR
2 TEASPOONS BAKING POWDER
1 TEASPOON SALT
1 CUP MILK
1/4 CUP VEGETABLE OIL
2 EGGS, LIGHTLY BEATEN
1/2 CUP CANNED CORN

Combine cornmeal, flour, sugar, baking powder and salt. Add milk, oil and eggs. Beat until smooth. Stir in corn. Spoon batter into greased muffin pan cups. Bake at 400 degrees for 15 to 20 minutes. Makes 8 to 12.

HOT CHOCOLATE

3 CUPS MILK
1/3 TO 1/2 CUP CHOCOLATE-FLAVORED SYRUP
WHIPPED CREAM (OPTIONAL)
MARSHMALLOWS (OPTIONAL)
CINNAMON STICK CANDY (OPTIONAL)

Heat milk in saucepan over medium heat until hot but not boiling. Stir in syrup. Pour into mugs and serve with whipped cream, marshmallows or candy sticks. For microwave preparation, pour milk into 4-cup microwave-safe measure. Microwave, uncovered, at high setting (100%) for 5 to 6 minutes or until hot. Blend in syrup. Serves 4.

PARTY PINWHEELS

1 (8 OUNCE) CAN REFRIGERATED CRESCENT ROLLS
4 (4X7") OR 8 (3 3/4x3 3/4") THIN SLICES HAM
1 TABLESPOON PLUS 1 TEASPOON PREPARED MUSTARD
1 CUP (4 OUNCES) SHREDDED SWISS OR CHEDDAR CHEESE
2 TABLESPOONS SESAME SEEDS

Separate dough into 4 long rectangles. Press perforations to seal. Place ham on rectangles, spread with mustard and sprinkle with cheese. Starting from short side, roll rectangles, jelly roll style, and press edges to seal. Coat rolls with sesame seed. Cut each roll into 5 slices and place, cut side down, on ungreased baking sheet. Bake at 375 degrees for 15 to 20 minutes or until golden brown. Makes 20.

APPLE SLICES WITH DIP

1 (8 OUNCE) CARTON SOUR CREAM
1 TABLESPOON SUGAR
1/2 TEASPOON PUMPKIN PIE SPICE
1/4 TEASPOON VANILLA
4 MEDIUM APPLES

Combine sour cream, sugar, pie spice and vanilla. Chill, covered, until ready to serve. Cut apples into wedges for dipping. Makes 1 cup.

FUN-FLAVORED POPCORN
SEASONED POPCORN

MELTED BUTTER
2 QUARTS POPPED CORN
SEASONED SALT
GRATED AMERICAN CHEESE
DRY SOUP MIX
BACON FLAVORED BITS

MEXICALI POPCORN

3 TABLESPOONS BUTTER
2 QUARTS POPPED CORN
1 1/2 TEASPOONS TACO SEASONING MIX
1 1/2 TEASPOONS DRIED CHOPPED CHIVES
SALT TO TASTE

PEANUT BUTTER POPCORN

2 TABLESPOONS BUTTER OR MARGARINE
2 QUARTS POPPED CORN
1 TABLESPOON CREAMY OR CHUNKY PEANUT BUTTER

For SEASONED POPCORN, drizzle butter over popped corn and add seasoned salt, cheese, soup mix or bacon bits or a combination. For MEXICALI POPCORN, melt butter over low heat. Stir in taco seasoning and chives. Drizzle over popped corn and season to taste with salt. For PEANUT BUTTER POPCORN, melt butter with peanut butter in small saucepan, blending until smooth. Pour over popped corn, mix well and season to taste with salt. Makes 2 quarts.

VIDEO CAKE

3/4 CUP BUTTER, SOFTENED
1 2/3 CUPS SUGAR
3 EGGS
1 TEASPOON VANILLA
2 CUPS ALL-PURPOSE FLOUR
2/3 CUP COCOA
1/4 TEASPOON BAKING POWDER
1 1/4 TEASPOONS BAKING SODA
1 TEASPOON SALT
1 1/3 CUPS WATER
MINIATURE MARSHMALLOWS
1 TUBE WHITE PREPARED FROSTING
CHOCOLATE FROSTING:
3 CUPS POWDERED SUGAR
1/2 CUP COCOA
1/2 CUP BUTTER, SOFTENED
5 TO 6 TABLESPOONS MILK
1 TEASPOON VANILLA

Cream butter and sugar together until smooth. Add eggs and vanilla, beating until light. Sift flour, cocoa, baking powder, baking soda and salt together. Alternately add dry ingredients and water to creamed mixture, blending just until combined. Pour batter into greased and floured 13x9x2" baking pan. Bake at 350 degrees for 30 to 35 minutes. Cool in pan for 10 minutes, then remove to wire rack to complete cooling. Prepare frosting by combining 1 cup powdered sugar, cocoa, butter, 2 tablespoons milk and vanilla. Beat until creamy. Gradually add remaining powdered sugar alternately with remaining milk, beating until smooth. Place cake on platter or foil-covered cardboard. Spread chocolate frosting smoothly on top and sides of cake. Arrange marshmallows in row on each long side of cake to resemble holes in strip of film. Using tube of frosting, write a birthday "movie title" such as "Happy Birthday #(age)" and then "Starring (child's name)". Serves 12 to 16.

SHIRLEY TEMPLES

1 (8 TO 10 OUNCE) JAR MARASCHINO CHERRIES WITH STEMS
2 (1 LITER) BOTTLES GINGER ALE, CHILLED
8 FRESH ORANGE SLICES

Pour 1 tablespoon cherry juice and 2 cherries into each of 8 glasses. Fill with ginger ale and garnish with orange slice. For ROB ROY, substitute chilled cola soft drink for ginger ale. Serves 8.

SURPRISE BURGERS

1 1/2 POUNDS GROUND BEEF
1 CUP SOFT BREADCRUMBS
1 TABLESPOON PLUS 1 TEASPOON PREPARED MUSTARD
2 CLOVES GARLIC, CRUSHED
1/4 TEASPOON SALT
DASH OF BLACK PEPPER
1/4 CUP MILK
2 (10 OUNCE) PACKAGES SWISS CHEESE
8 FRENCH ROLLS
LEAF LETTUCE (OPTIONAL)
RED BELL PEPPER STRIPS (OPTIONAL)

Combine beef, breadcrumbs, mustard, garlic, salt, black pepper and milk, mixing well. Cut each chunk of cheese lengthwise into 4 slices. Wrap portion of meat mixture around each cheese slice. Place in 13x9x2" baking pan. Bake at 400 degrees for 10 to 15 minutes or until cheese begins to melt. While burgers bake, split rolls lengthwise and toast. Place burgers in rolls and garnish with lettuce and bell pepper strips. Serves 8.

MYSTERY SALAD

1 HEAD LETTUCE, SHREDDED
2 MEDIUM RED ONIONS, SLICED
1 TO 2 GREEN BELL PEPPERS, SLICED
3 TO 4 STALKS CELERY, CHOPPED
1 (8 OUNCE) CAN WATER CHESTNUTS, SLICED
1 (10 OUNCE) PACKAGE FROZEN GREEN PEAS
2 CUPS MAYONNAISE
GRATED PARMESAN CHEESE
3 HARD-COOKED EGGS, SLICED
4 SLICES BACON, COOKED AND CRUMBLED
1 TO 2 TOMATOES, SLICED

In large opaque bowl, layer ingredients in order: lettuce, onion, bell pepper, celery, water chestnuts and peas. Spread mayonnaise over layer of peas, covering to edges. Sprinkle with cheese. Do not mix ingredients. Chill, covered, for 24 hours. Remove from refrigerator 45 minutes before serving. Garnish with egg slices, bacon and tomato slices. Serves 12 to 14.

Make an easy decorating bag for writing on cakes and cookies by cutting the corner off a plastic bag and partially filling it with frosting. Write with frosting by gently squeezing the frosting through the hole.

CUPCAKES WITH A SECRET

1 (8 OUNCE) PACKAGE CREAM CHEESE, SOFTENED
1 EGG, LIGHTLY BEATEN
1/3 CUP SUGAR
1/8 TEASPOON SALT
1 (6 OUNCE) PACKAGE CHOCOLATE CHIPS
1 (18 1/2 OUNCE) PACKAGE CHOCOLATE CAKE MIX

Combine cream cheese, egg, sugar and salt, mixing well. Stir in chocolate chips and set aside. Prepare cake mix according to package directions. Spoon batter into paper-lined muffin pan cups, filling 1/3 to 1/2 full. Drop a rounded teaspoonful of cream cheese mixture in center of each cupcake. Bake at 350 degrees for 20 to 25 minutes. Cupcakes can be served without frosting or frosted and decorated with letters to spell out "Happy Birthday" or with question marks. Makes 24 to 28.

PAINTED PUNCH

3 FLAVORS POWDERED DRINK MIX
LEMON-LIME CARBONATED SOFT DRINK

Prepare different flavors of drink mix. Pour into separate ice cube trays and freeze. Float cubes in lemon-lime soft drink in punch bowl.

PIRATE SHIPS

4 SMALL CLUB ROLLS
1 1/2 CUPS DICED HAM
1/3 CUP CHOPPED CELERY
3 TABLESPOONS MAYONNAISE OR SALAD DRESSING
2 TABLESPOONS CHOPPED GREEN ONION
1 TEASPOON LEMON JUICE
DASH OF BLACK PEPPER
2 SLICES AMERICAN CHEESE

Split rolls lengthwise. Scoop out center of each, leaving a 1/4" shell. Combine ham, celery, mayonnaise or salad dressing, onion, lemon juice and black pepper. Spoon filling into center of roll halves. Cut cheese slices into quarters. Thread each piece on wooden pick and insert in filling for "sail". Serves 4-8.

GOLD COINS

3/4 CUP ALL-PURPOSE FLOUR
1 (5 OUNCE) JAR AMERICAN CHEESE SPREAD
1/4 CUP BUTTER OR MARGARINE, SOFTENED
1 CUP CORN FLAKES, FINELY CRUSHED (1/2 CUP)

Combine flour, cheese spread and butter or margarine, mixing with hands until well combined. Spread crushed corn flakes on waxed paper. Shape cheese mixture into 1" balls by rolling small portions between palms, roll in corn flakes and place about 2" apart on ungreased baking sheet. Using bottom of drinking glass, flatten balls to 1/4" thickness. Bake at 375 degrees for about 12 minutes or until edges are lightly browned. Makes 18 to 20.

WALK THE PLANK SNACKS

CELERY STALKS
PEANUT BUTTER
RAISINS

Cut celery stalks into 2" pieces. Spread peanut butter in groove of each piece. Place several raisins on peanut butter for "footprints" along "plank".

TREASURE CHEST CAKE

1 LOAF POUND CAKE
PEANUT BUTTER FROSTING (PAGE 127)
1 KNOT SHAPE PRETZEL
4 LICORICE LACES
1 TO 2 MILK CHOCOLATE CANDY BARS
LIGHT BROWN SUGAR
ASSORTED CANDIES

Spread cake with frosting. Press pretzel in middle of front side for lock. Arrange 2 licorice laces along each end of top of cake and 2 squares of chocolate at corners of each side for trim. Place on serving plate. Sprinkle plate with brown sugar to resemble sand and scatter candies around cake for coins and jewels. Serves 8.

PASTA SALAD

1 (8 OUNCE) PACKAGE RAINBOW ROTINI PASTA
2 CUPS BROCCOLI FLOWERETS
1 1/2 CUPS SLICED FRESH MUSHROOMS
1 1/2 CUPS CHERRY TOMATO HALVES OR QUARTERS
1 (3 OUNCE) CAN SLICED RIPE OLIVES, DRAINED
1/2 CUP QUARTERED PEPPERONI SLICES
1/2 CUP SLICED CARROTS
1 TABLESPOON GRATED PARMESAN CHEESE
1 (8 OUNCE) BOTTLE ZESTY ITALIAN SALAD DRESSING

Prepare pasta according to package directions. Rinse with cold water and drain well. Combine pasta, broccoli, mushrooms, tomatoes, olives, pepperoni, carrots and cheese. Gradually add salad dressing, tossing to coat thoroughly. Serves 10 to 12.

. . . .

CREAM PUFFS

1 CUP BOILING WATER
1/2 CUP VEGETABLE SHORTENING
1 CUP ALL-PURPOSE FLOUR
4 EGGS
WHIPPED CREAM OR INSTANT PUDDING, PREPARED

Combine boiling water and shortening in saucepan. Bring to a boil. Stir in flour, mixing thoroughly, and remove from heat. Let stand to cool slightly. Add eggs, 1 at a time, beating well after each addition. Drop dough by spoonfuls about 2" apart on greased baking sheet, shaping into slightly mounded circles. Bake at 400 degrees for 15 minutes, reduce oven temperature to 350 degrees and bake for 45 minutes. Let puffs stand until cool. Cut slit in side of each puff and fill with whipped cream or pudding. Serve immediately. Unfilled puffs can be stored in freezer. Makes 40 to 50 small puffs or 10 to 12 large puffs.

BAKED POTATO PLANES

6 BAKING POTATOES
1 1/2 CUPS SOUR CREAM
1/4 CUP BUTTER
2 TABLESPOONS CHIVES (OPTIONAL)
SALT AND BLACK PEPPER TO TASTE
BACON BITS (OPTIONAL)
GRATED CHEESE (OPTIONAL)
24 CARROT STICKS
12 BROCCOLI FLOWERETS

Bake potatoes at 400 degrees for 1 hour or until done. Let stand until cool enough to handle. Cut potatoes lengthwise. Scoop out pulp and place in mixing bowl; reserve potato shells. Add sour cream, butter, chives, salt and black pepper. Mash until thoroughly blended. Spoon potato mixture into potato shells. Sprinkle with bacon and cheese. Place on baking sheet and bake at 350 degrees for 10 minutes. Insert carrot stick on each side of each potato half for wings and broccoli floweret at one end for the propeller. Serves 12.

MIXED FRUIT IN A PLANE-SHAPED WATERMELON

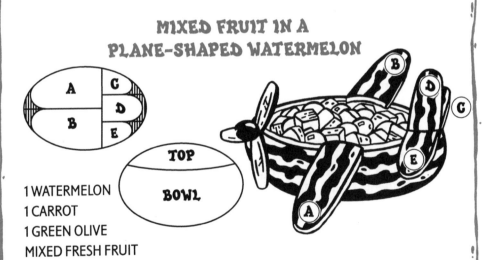

1 WATERMELON
1 CARROT
1 GREEN OLIVE
MIXED FRESH FRUIT

Cutting lengthwise, remove top 1/3 of watermelon. Scoop pulp from watermelon, cutting into bite-sized pieces. Following the diagram, cut wings and tail from top piece of rind. Attach to the watermelon bowl with wooden picks, trimming slightly if too thick or heavy. Cut 3 strips from carrot for propeller and attach to front end of plane with wooden pick. Cover end of pick with olive. Combine watermelon chunks and other favorite fruits and place in "airplane" to serve. Serves 12 to 16.

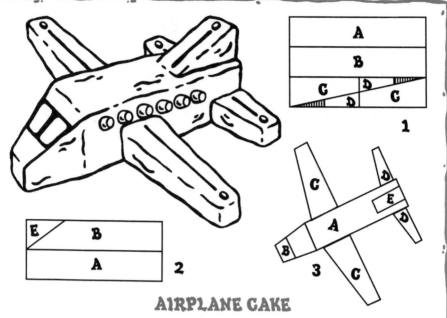

AIRPLANE CAKE

1 (18 1/2 OUNCE) PACKAGE CAKE MIX
3 1/2 CUPS WHITE FROSTING (PAGE 137)
BLUE FOOD COLORING

Prepare cake mix according to package directions. Bake in 13x9x2" baking pan.
Cool in pan for 10 minutes, then remove to wire rack to complete cooling. Tint
1/2 cup frosting with blue food coloring. Reserve for decorating cake. Place cake
on wax paper on flat surface. Trim top and edges of cake, then cut according to
diagram 1. Place piece A in center of 19x13" covered cake board and spread top
with white frosting. Place piece B on frosting. Beginning 3" from 1 end, make
an angled cut in piece B, as shown in diagram 2. Arrange remaining pieces as
shown in diagram 3, using frosting to join sections. Trim "nose" end to about
1" wide and trim top side edges of piece B for rounded shape. Spread frosting on
all surfaces of assembled cake. Using a writing tip and tinted frosting, pipe
outlines for windows and design on wings. Serves 12 to 16.

PROPELLER PUNCH

2 QUARTS CRANBERRY-APPLE DRINK
3 CUPS UNSWEETENED PINEAPPLE JUICE
2 TEASPOONS FRESH LEMON JUICE
1 QUART GINGER ALE, CHILLED
1 PINT RASPBERRY SHERBET

Combine cranberry-apple drink, pineapple juice and lemon juice in large pitcher.
Chill for at least 2 hours before serving. Add ginger ale just before serving. Pour
punch into glasses, filling 3/4 full. Place small scoop of sherbet in each glass.
Serves 12 to 15.

PIZZA CASSEROLE

1 (8 OUNCE) PACKAGE MACARONI
1 POUND GROUND TURKEY
1 SMALL ONION, FINELY CHOPPED
1/2 MEDIUM-SIZED GREEN BELL PEPPER, FINELY CHOPPED
1 (14 OUNCE) JAR PIZZA SAUCE
1/2 TEASPOON GARLIC SALT
1 1/2 CUPS (6 OUNCES) SHREDDED PIZZA CHEESE, DIVIDED
1 (3 1/2 OUNCE) PACKAGE SLICED PEPPERONI

Prepare macaroni according to package directions. While macaroni cooks, brown turkey with onion and bell pepper in large skillet over medium heat, stirring to crumble meat. Drain excess fat. Stir in pizza sauce, garlic salt, well-drained macaroni and 1 cup cheese. Spoon mixture into lightly-greased 13x9x2" baking pan. Arrange pepperoni on macaroni mixture. Bake, covered, at 350 degrees for 25 to 30 minutes or until thoroughly heated; sprinkle with remaining cheese and bake for additional 5 minutes. Serves 8.

GARLIC BREAD

1/2 CUP BUTTER OR MARGARINE, SOFTENED
1/4 CUP (1 OUNCE) GRATED PARMESAN CHEESE
2 CLOVES GARLIC, PRESSED
1/4 TEASPOON DRIED MARJORAM
1/4 TEASPOON DRIED OREGANO
1 (16 OUNCE) LOAF FRENCH BREAD

Combine butter or margarine, cheese, garlic, marjoram and oregano. Cut bread in half horizontally. Spread cut surfaces with seasoned butter. Reassemble loaf, wrap in aluminum foil and place on a baking sheet. Bake at 350 degrees for 20 minutes; for crispy crust, open foil and bake for additional 5 minutes. Slice and serve. Serves 8.

CHAMPION BROWNIES

2 EGGS
1 CUP SUGAR
1/2 CUP BUTTER, MELTED
2 (1 OUNCE) SQUARES CHOCOLATE, MELTED, OR 7 TABLESPOONS COCOA
PLUS 1 TABLESPOON MARGARINE
1 TEASPOON VANILLA
1/2 CUP ALL-PURPOSE FLOUR
PINCH OF SALT
1 CUP CHOPPED NUTS (OPTIONAL)

Beat eggs. Add sugar and beat until smooth. Combine melted butter and chocolate; stir in egg mixture. Blend in vanilla. Sift flour and salt together and add to chocolate mixture, beating until smooth. Add nuts. Pour batter into greased 9x9x2" baking pan. Bake at 350 degrees for 25 to 30 minutes. Makes 12 to 16.

AWARD WINNING PUNCH

1 (12 OUNCE) CAN FROZEN ORANGE JUICE CONCENTRATE, THAWED
1 (12 OUNCE) CAN FROZEN LEMONADE CONCENTRATE, THAWED
2 (46 OUNCE) CANS RED FRUIT PUNCH DRINK
1 (2 LITER) BOTTLE GINGER ALE

Combine undiluted orange juice and lemonade concentrates and fruit punch in large plastic container. Chill until ready to serve. Stir in ginger ale and serve over ice. Makes 5 quarts.

HEART PIZZA

1/2 POUND GROUND BEEF OR SAUSAGE OR 1 (3 1/2 OUNCE) PACKAGE
PEPPERONI SLICES
1 (10 OUNCE) PACKAGE REFRIGERATED PIZZA DOUGH
1 (14 1/2 OUNCE) JAR PIZZA SAUCE
1 TO 2 CUPS (4 TO 8 OUNCES) SHREDDED OR SLICED MOZZARELLA CHEESE
2 CUPS CHOPPED COOKED VEGETABLES

Cook beef or sausage until browned; drain excess fat. Unroll dough and divide into
four portions. Shape each portion into heart and place on greased baking sheet. Spread
sauce on dough. In order, sprinkle cheese, vegetables and meat on sauce. Bake at 425
degrees according to package directions or until bottom surfaces of pizzas are golden
brown. Serves 4.

. . . .

HUGS AND KISSES

1/4 CUP BUTTER OR MARGARINE, MELTED
1 TABLESPOON WORCESTERSHIRE SAUCE
1 TEASPOON SEASONED SALT
1 CUP PRETZEL STICKS (BITE SIZED LENGTHS)
8 CUPS RICE, CORN OR WHEAT SQUARE CEREAL
CANDY-COATED CHOCOLATE CANDIES, RAISINS, MINIATURE
MARSHMALLOWS, BUTTERSCOTCH MORSELS, CHOCOLATE CHIPS OR PEANUT
BUTTER MORSELS (OPTIONAL)

Combine butter or margarine, Worcestershire sauce and seasoned salt, mixing well.
Combine pretzels and cereal in large bowl. Drizzle seasoned butter over cereal mixture
and mix gently until evenly coated. Spread mixture in 14x10x3" baking pan. Bake at
300 degrees for 1 hour, stirring at 15 minute intervals. Spread mixture on paper towels
to cool. Add 1 cup of one or several of optional ingredients. Makes 10 to 12 cups.

. . . .

HEARTS GALORE PARFAIT

1 (1/4 OUNCE) PACKAGE PINK LEMONADE DRINK MIX
1 CUP SUGAR
COLD WATER
4 PACKETS UNFLAVORED GELATIN
4 RED GUMMIE CANDY HEARTS
WHIPPED CREAM
SPRINKLES

Combine lemonade, sugar and water according to package directions. Sprinkle gelatin into 1 cup cold lemonade mixture and let stand for 1 minute. Heat remaining 3 cups lemonade and add to gelatin liquid, stirring until completely dissolved. Pour 1 cup lemonade mixture into each serving glass. Chill for 50 minutes or until partially thickened (if too thin, continue chilling and checking at 5 minute intervals). Drop candy heart into each glass; heart should be suspended midway in gelatin. Chill for additional 30 minutes until completely firm. Garnish with whipped cream and sprinkles. Serves 4.

. . . .

DOUBLE HEART COOKIES

1 (20 OUNCE) PACKAGE REFRIGERATED SUGAR COOKIE DOUGH
1 (16 OUNCE) CAN WHITE FROSTING
RED FOOD COLORING
POWDERED SUGAR
15 CINNAMON HEARTS (OPTIONAL)

Prepare dough according to package directions for cut-out cookies. Using heart-shaped cutter, cut approximately 30 hearts from dough. Using a sharp knife or smaller cutter, cut small heart from center of half of hearts. Place on ungreased baking sheet. Bake at 350 degrees for 7 to 9 minutes. Cool on wire rack. Tint frosting with food coloring to pink shade. Spread frosting on each solid heart cookie, top with cut-out cookie and sprinkle with powdered sugar. Place cinnamon heart in center of each assembled cookie. Makes 15.

HAPPY HEARTS CAKE

1 (18 1/2 OUNCE) PACKAGE YELLOW CAKE MIX
1 (16 OUNCE) CAN WHITE FROSTING
RED FOOD COLORING
RED HOTS OR VALENTINE CANDIES

Prepare cake mix according to package directions, baking in a 9" round baking pan and 8x8x2" baking pan. Cool in pans for 10 minutes, then remove to wire rack to complete cooling. Cut and assemble cake according to illustration. Tint frosting with food coloring to pink shade. Spread frosting on cake. Decorate with candies. Serves 12 to 15.

SWEETHEART STRAWBERRY DAIQUIRIS

1 (6 OUNCE) CAN FROZEN LEMONADE CONCENTRATE
1 (6 OUNCE) CAN WATER
1 PINT FRESH STRAWBERRIES, HULLED, OR FROZEN STRAWBERRIES
ICE

Combine lemonade concentrate, water and strawberries in blender container. Add ice and blend until smooth and slushy. Serves 6.

EGG SHAPED SANDWICHES

1 (10 OUNCE) PACKAGE FROZEN STRAWBERRIES, THAWED AND DRAINED

1 (8 OUNCE) PACKAGE CREAM CHEESE, SOFTENED

1 TABLESPOON SUGAR

16 SLICES WHITE SANDWICH BREAD

Combine strawberries, cream cheese and sugar in food processor bowl or blender. Process until well blended. Spread mixture on half of bread slices, top with second slices and cut sandwich in egg shape, using cookie cutter or sharp knife tip. Serves 8.

> Use a *clean*, empty frozen juice concentrate can pushed into an oval shape to make egg shaped sandwiches or cookies.

EGG NEST TREATS

1 (6 OUNCE) PACKAGE SEMI-SWEET CHOCOLATE CHIPS

1 (6 OUNCE) PACKAGE BUTTERSCOTCH CHIPS

1 (5 OUNCE) CAN CHOW MEIN NOODLES

JELLY BEANS

Combine chocolate and butterscotch chips in microwave-safe bowl. Microwave at high (100% setting) until chips are melted. Stir until smooth. Stir in noodles and mix until well coated. Drop mixture by teaspoonfuls on wax paper, shaping each to form "nest". Place jelly bean eggs in each and let stand until cool. Makes 18 to 24.

BUNNY CAKE

1 (18 1/2 OUNCE) PACKAGE CAKE MIX

1 (16 OUNCE) CAN WHITE FROSTING

RED FOOD COLORING

FLAKED COCONUT

LICORICE LACES

JELLY BEANS

Prepare cake mix according to package directions, baking in 2 round 9" baking pans. Cool in pans for 10 minutes, then remove to wire rack to complete cooling. Cut 1 layer according to illustration. Assemble cake pieces to form bunny head. Tint small amount of frosting to pink shade. Spread pink frosting in center of ears. Spread white frosting on remainder of face and ears; frost bow tie with either white or pink frosting. Sprinkle coconut on face and ears. Arrange licorice and other candies on frosting for facial features and pattern on bow tie. Serves 12 to 16.

BAR-B-QUED CHICKEN

1 LARGE ONION, DICED
2 TABLESPOONS BUTTER
2 LARGE CLOVES GARLIC, MINCED
2 TABLESPOONS WATER
1/4 CUP FIRMLY-PACKED BROWN SUGAR
1 CUP KETCHUP
2 TABLESPOONS WHITE VINEGAR
1 TABLESPOON PREPARED DIJON MUSTARD
2 TABLESPOONS WORCESTERSHIRE SAUCE
1 TEASPOON GRATED ORANGE PEEL
1/4 CUP ORANGE JUICE
10 PIECES CHICKEN

Sauté onion in butter until soft, add garlic and cook until onion is translucent. Stir in water and brown sugar and simmer for 1 minute. Using wooden spoon and stirring constantly, add ketchup, vinegar, mustard, Worcestershire sauce and orange peel. Gradually add orange juice and blend. Simmer for 15 to 20 minutes, stirring occasionally. Grill chicken according to preferred method, brushing pieces with sauce several times. Makes 2 cups sauce. Serves 5.

POTATO SALAD

5 CUPS QUARTERED POTATOES
WATER
SALT
1/2 CUP MAYONNAISE
1 TEASPOON SALT
1/4 TEASPOON BLACK PEPPER
1 TEASPOON PREPARED MUSTARD
2 HARD-COOKED EGGS
1 MEDIUM ONION, MINCED
4 OR 5 STALKS CELERY, FINELY CHOPPED
1/2 CUP SWEET PICKLE RELISH
PAPRIKA

Cook potatoes in boiling salted water until tender. Drain well. Combine mayonnaise, 1 teaspoon salt, black pepper, mustard and yolk of cooked eggs, mixing well. Combine onion, celery, relish and chopped white of eggs; add to potatoes. Fold mayonnaise mixture into potatoes. Spoon into serving dish and garnish with paprika. Chill for 2 hours and serve cold. Serves 8 to 10.

ROASTED CORN

12 EARS CORN WITH HUSKS
1/2 CUP BUTTER
SALT AND BLACK PEPPER

Soak corn with husks in water for 15 minutes. Remove and place directly on hot grill. Grill for 8 to 16 minutes, turning to cook evenly. Remove from grill, carefully remove husks, spread with butter and season with salt and black pepper. Serves 12.

FRUIT PIZZA

1 (20 OUNCE) PACKAGE REFRIGERATED SUGAR COOKIE DOUGH
1 (8 OUNCE) PACKAGE CREAM CHEESE, SOFTENED
1 (12 OUNCE) CONTAINER FROZEN WHIPPED TOPPING, THAWED
1/2 CUP SUGAR
FRESH STRAWBERRIES
BANANA SLICES
FRESH PEACH CHUNKS
CANNED PINEAPPLE CHUNKS, DRAINED

Cut cookie dough roll in 1/2" slices. Arrange on 12" pizza pan and press edges to form solid crust. Bake at 350 degrees for 15 to 20 minutes or until light golden brown. Combine cream cheese, whipped topping and sugar, mixing until smooth. Spread filling on cooled crust. Arrange strawberries, bananas, peaches and pineapple in rings on filling. Serves 8 to 12.

TASTY LEMONADE

6 LARGE LEMONS
1 CUP SUGAR
2 QUARTS COLD WATER

Squeeze juice from lemons into measuring cup (should yield 1 1/2 cups juice). Remove any seeds. Combine juice, sugar and water in large pitcher and serve over ice. Makes 2 1/2 quarts.

For more juice, roll lemons on a countertop, pressing firmly, before slicing and squeezing.

RED, WHITE AND BLUE POPS

4 CUPS RASPBERRY-FLAVORED FRUIT DRINK
2 CUPS WATER, DIVIDED
1 PINT VANILLA FROZEN YOGURT
3/4 CUP FRESH OR FROZEN BLUEBERRIES
10 ICE CREAM STICKS

Pour 1" raspberry drink into each of 10 five-ounce plastic drink cups. Place in baking pan and place in freezer. When liquid is partially frozen, place an ice cream stick upright in center of each cup and return to freezer. Combine 1 cup water and 4 large scoops yogurt in blender container. Blend until smooth. Pour 1" yogurt mix on frozen raspberry layer and return to freezer. Combine 1 cup water, blueberries and 1 large scoop yogurt in blender container. Blend until smooth. Spoon mixture on yogurt layer. Freeze overnight. Dip each cup briefly into warm water to loosen so pop can be easily removed. Serves 10.

SPIDER SANDWICHES

24 SLICES WHEAT SANDWICH BREAD
1 1/2 CUPS CREAMY PEANUT BUTTER
24 RAISINS
1 (6 1/2 OUNCE) CAN CHEESE CURLS

Using a 2 1/2" round cutter, cut a circle from each bread slice. Spread about 2 tablespoons peanut butter on half of bread rounds and top with remaining bread rounds. Make 2 small indentations on top of each sandwich for "eyes". Press raisin into each, using small amount of peanut butter to secure. Store sandwiches in shallow container, covered with plastic wrap and topped with a damp dish towel, in the refrigerator until ready to serve. Just before serving, place sandwiches on tray and insert 8 cheese curls into each for legs. Serves 12.

GOBLINS GOOP

1 (15 OUNCE) CAN UNSWEETENED PINEAPPLE CHUNKS, DRAINED
1 (11 OUNCE) CAN MANDARIN ORANGES, DRAINED
1/2 CUP FLAKED COCONUT
1/2 CUP WALNUTS OR PECANS (OPTIONAL)
3 TABLESPOONS MAYONNAISE
WHIPPED TOPPING
1/2 TO 1 CUP MINIATURE MARSHMALLOWS

Combine pineapple, oranges, coconut and walnuts or pecans. Stir in mayonnaise with just enough whipped topping to moisten. Fold in marshmallows. Chill before serving. Serves 8 to 10.

JACK-O-LANTERN TREATS

1/4 CUP MARGARINE
1 (10 OUNCE) PACKAGE MARSHMALLOWS
5 CUPS CRISPY RICE CEREAL
BUTTER CREAM FROSTING (PAGE 120)
CANDY CORN

Melt margarine in large saucepan over low heat. Add marshmallows, stir until melted and blended and cook for 3 additional minutes, stirring constantly. Remove from heat. Stir in cereal and mix until well coated. Divide in 10 portions. To make jack-o-lanterns, shape each into slightly mounded circles to resemble pumpkins. Spread with frosting and decorate with candy corn for eyes, noses and mouths. Makes 10.

ICE CREAM PUMPKINS

1 GALLON ORANGE SHERBET
CANDY CORN OR OTHER CANDIES

At least 24 hours before serving, shape large scoops of sherbet into firm, well-rounded balls. Place on baking sheet. Arrange candy pieces on 1 side of each ball to form jack-o-lantern features. Freeze, uncovered, until 10 to 15 minutes before serving. Just before serving, insert a small yellow birthday candle in top of each jack-o-lantern and light. Serves 12 to 16.

JACK-O-LANTERN CAKE

2 (18 1/2 OUNCE) PACKAGES CAKE MIX
2 (16 OUNCE) CANS WHITE FROSTING
RED FOOD COLORING
YELLOW FOOD COLORING
LICORICE LACES
1 (12 OUNCE) PACKAGE CANDY CORN OR OTHER
HALLOWEEN CANDIES

Prepare cake mixes according to package directions. Bake in 2 greased 10" fluted tube pans at 350 degrees for 40 to 45 minutes or until wooden pick inserted near centers comes out clean. Cool for 10 minutes in pans, then remove to wire rack to complete cooling. Using sharp knife, trim bottom of cakes to lie flat. Invert 1 cake, flat side up. Tint frosting with food colorings to orange shade. Spread on cut surface of cake and top with second cake, flat side down. Spread frosting on all surfaces of assembled cake. Decorate with licorice laces to make a jack-o-lantern face and fill center with candies. Serves 24 to 30.

WITCHES BREW

1 QUART APPLE JUICE
1 1/2 CUPS UNSWEETENED PINEAPPLE JUICE
2 TABLESPOONS LEMON JUICE
2 TABLESPOONS HONEY
3 CINNAMON STICKS

Combine apple, pineapple and lemon juices, honey and cinnamon sticks in large saucepan. Simmer until steaming hot. Remove cinnamon sticks before serving. Serves 8.

POTATO LATKES

3 BAKING POTATOES, PEELED
1/2 TO 1 ONION
SALT AND BLACK PEPPER TO TASTE
1 EGG, BEATEN
1/4 CUP ALL-PURPOSE FLOUR
VEGETABLE OIL

Grate potatoes and onion (To avoid discoloration, do not grate potatoes in advance). Mix with salt, black pepper, egg and flour. Pour oil into skillet to 1/4" depth and heat until very hot. Drop spoonfuls of potato mixture into oil, flattening slightly. Fry, turning once, until golden brown on both sides. Place on paper towels to drain excess oil. Serve with applesauce, sour cream or both. Makes 10 to 12.

DOUGHNUTS

2 (8 OUNCE) CANS REFRIGERATED BISCUITS
1/4 CUP JAM OR JELLY
VEGETABLE OIL
SUPERFINE GRANULATED SUGAR

Separate biscuit pieces and press to flatten slightly. Spread 1 teaspoon jam or jelly in center of 10 biscuit rounds, top each with remaining biscuit piece and press edges to seal. Pour oil into electric skillet to 1/2 its depth or use regular skillet. Heat to 380 degrees. Carefully slip dough pockets into oil and cook, turning once, until golden brown on each side. Place on paper towels to drain excess oil, cool and roll in sugar. Makes 10.

HANUKKAH COOKIES

2 CUPS SUGAR
1/4 CUP FIRMLY-PACKED LIGHT BROWN SUGAR
1 CUP BUTTER
2 EGGS
1/4 CUP PLUS 2 TABLESPOONS MILK
2 TEASPOONS VANILLA
4 CUPS ALL-PURPOSE FLOUR
2 TEASPOONS BAKING POWDER
1/2 TEASPOON SALT

Cream sugar, brown sugar and butter together until smooth. Add eggs, milk and vanilla and beat thoroughly. Combine flour, baking powder and salt. Add to creamed mixture and beat until blended. Chill dough. Roll to 1/8" thickness, cut with Hanukkah symbol cutters and place on greased baking sheets. Bake at 350 degrees for 10 to 12 minutes or until golden brown. Makes 60.

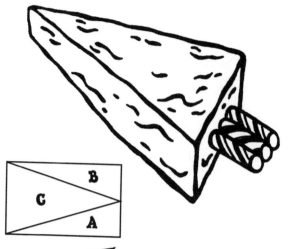

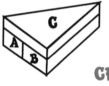

When serving a decorated cake, make sure there are enough decorations on it for each child to get some. If not, have some extras ready to serve.

CHRISTMAS TREE CAKE

1 (18 1/2 OUNCE) PACKAGE YELLOW CAKE MIX
2 TABLESPOONS GREEN DECORATOR SUGAR
2 TABLESPOONS MULTI-COLORED TINY DECORATOR CANDIES
1 (16 OUNCE) CAN WHITE FROSTING
GREEN DECORATOR SUGAR
3 PEPPERMINT STICKS

Prepare cake mix according to package directions. Pour batter into greased 13x9x2" baking pan . Sprinkle with 2 tablespoons green sugar and multicolor candies, swirl with knife tip to distribute through batter and bake according to package directions. Cool in pan for 10 minutes, then remove to wire rack to complete cooling. Cut and assemble cake as shown in illustration. Use frosting to hold pieces together. Spread frosting on assembled cake, swirling with spatula tip to simulate branches. Sprinkle entire cake with green sugar. Insert tips of peppermint sticks at base of tree for trunk. Serves 12 to 16.

CINNAMON CIDER

4 CUPS CIDER OR APPLE JUICE
1/4 CUP CINNAMON RED HOT CANDIES

Combine cider or juice and candies in large saucepan. Bring to a boil, reduce heat and simmer for 4 minutes or until candies are dissolved. Serve hot or cold. Serves 8.

KWANZAA SPICY CHICKEN

1/4 CUP HOT SAUCE
1 TABLESPOON MUSTARD
6 BONELESS CHICKEN BREAST HALVES
1 CUP ALL-PURPOSE FLOUR
1 TABLESPOON CORNMEAL
1/4 CUP ITALIAN SEASONED BREADCRUMBS
1 TEASPOON BAKING POWDER
1/2 CUP VEGETABLE OIL

Combine hot sauce and mustard in mixing bowl. Add chicken, turn to coat thoroughly and let stand for 10 minutes. Combine flour, cornmeal, breadcrumbs and baking powder in plastic bag. Add chicken and shake to coat well. Heat oil in heavy skillet until hot. Add chicken. Cook over high heat until lightly browned; reduce heat, cover and cook until almost crispy; remove cover and cook 3 additional minutes; turn chicken and cook over high heat until crispy and browned. Drain on paper towels. Serves 6.

CHEESY RICE BALLS

2 CUPS UNCOOKED BROWN RICE
4 CUPS (16 OUNCES) GRATED CHEDDAR CHEESE
4 EGGS, WELL BEATEN
4 CUPS ITALIAN SEASONED BREADCRUMBS

Prepare rice according to package directions. Immediately after rice is cooked, stir in cheese. Shape hot, sticky mixture into golf ball-sized balls. Dip balls in egg liquid, then coat with breadcrumbs. Fry in oil until golden brown on all sides. Makes about 48.

FRUIT SALAD

2 LEMONS

2 APPLES, CUBED

2 BANANAS, SLICED

2 KIWIS, PEELED AND SLICED

2 ORANGES, PEELED AND SECTIONED

1 CUP MELON CUBES

1 CUP SEEDLESS GRAPES

1/2 CUP WATER

1/4 CUP SUGAR

1/2 CUP CHOPPED NUTS

1/4 CUP FLAKED COCONUT

Extract juice from 1 lemon. Combine apples, bananas, kiwi, oranges, melon and grapes. Pour lemon juice over fruit to prevent discoloration. Combine water and sugar in saucepan. Heat until sugar is dissolved. Extract juice from second lemon and add to syrup. Boil for 2 minutes, remove from heat and let stand to cool. Pour cool syrup over fruit and mix well. Fold in nuts and coconut. Chill until ready to serve. Serves 6 to 8.

KARAMU COOKIES

1/2 CUP BUTTER, SOFTENED

1/2 CUP PEANUT BUTTER

1/2 CUP FIRMLY-PACKED BROWN SUGAR

1 TEASPOON VANILLA

1 EGG

1 1/2 CUPS ALL-PURPOSE FLOUR

1/2 TEASPOON BAKING SODA

1/2 TEASPOON SALT

FROSTING:

2 CUPS POWDERED SUGAR

1 TEASPOON VANILLA

3 TABLESPOONS WHIPPING CREAM, UNWHIPPED

BLACK, YELLOW, RED AND GREEN FOOD COLORING

Blend butter and peanut butter together. Add sugar and vanilla and beat until smooth. Blend in egg. Sift flour, baking soda and salt together. Add dry ingredients to peanut butter mixture and mix well. Divide dough into 2 portions. Shape each into a log. Cut in 1/4" slices and place on greased baking sheet. Bake at 400 degrees for 8 to 10 minutes. Cool cookies on wire rack. Prepare frosting by combining powdered sugar, vanilla and cream, beating until smooth. Tint portions of frosting with food coloring. Decorate cookies with African designs. Makes 48.

INDEX

INDEX

173

Virginia Hospitality

Elected to the Walter S. McIlhenney Hall of Fame for Community Cookbooks

Virginia Hospitality is a culinary tour capturing the hospitality, heritage and warmth that is Virginia.

• Mouth-watering recipes and tips from Virginia hostesses that reflect 200 years of gracious entertaining.

• 600 triple-tested no-fail recipes including Hot Virginia Dip, Islander Cheese Ball, Chesapeake Bay Crab Cakes and Tea Time Tassies from appetizers to desserts.

• Accompanying the recipes, pictorial histories of 26 famous Virginia homes with drawings by famous artists.

• Recipes from famous Virginia homes, resorts and restaurants, including The Homestead, the Williamsburg Inn and the Tides Inn.

• An award winning Junior League cookbook first published in 1975-now in its 15th printing with over 250,000 copies in print.

Very VIRGINIA
Culinary Traditions With A Twist

Between the pages of **Very Virginia**, you will find the best of Virginia's hospitality generously seasoned with contemporary flair.

• Over 400 triple-tested recipes emphasizing fresh ingredients and food indigenous to Virginia, such as Crab Mousse, Shenandoah Apple Muffins, Apricot Glazed Pork

Tenderloin, Sugar Coated Peanuts, Grilled Breast of Duck and many more.

• Seasonal menus for gracious entertaining with suggestions for wine accompaniment. Enjoy a Holiday Breakfast, Terrace Supper or Moonlight Cruise.

• An entire section devoted to pastas with appealing entrees such as Bow Ties with Smithfield Ham and Southern Shrimp and Pasta.

• Quick and easy favorites. Our Quick Raspberry Tart and Chesapeake Crab Spread are perfect for cooks on a tight schedule who like to serve wonderful dishes.

• Kids in the Kitchen! A section of child-tested favorites and delightful recipes to prepare with your children including Graham Cracker Brownies and Spaghetti Pie.

JUNIOR LEAGUE OF HAMPTON ROADS, INC.
729 Thimble Shoals Blvd., Ste. 4D • Newport News, Virginia 23606
Phone: (757) 873-0281 Fax: (757) 873-8747

Please send me _____ copies of **Children's Party Book**   @ \$13.95 each   \$ _____
Please send me _____ copies of **Virginia Hospitality**   @ \$15.95 each   \$ _____
Please send me _____ copies of **Very Virginia**   @ \$17.95 each   \$ _____
Shipping and Handling   @ \$3.50 each   \$ _____
Subtotal   \$ _____
Virginia residents add 4.5% tax   \$ _____
Total   \$ _____

Name _____

Address _____

City _____ State _____ Zip _____

Make checks payable to the Junior League of Hampton Roads, Inc.

(Payable in U.S. dollars only.)

Charge to: _____ Visa _____ Mastercard   Exp. Date _____

Card Number _____

Signature _____

JUNIOR LEAGUE OF HAMPTON ROADS, INC.
729 Thimble Shoals Blvd., Ste. 4D • Newport News, Virginia 23606
Phone: (757) 873-0281 Fax: (757) 873-8747

Please send me _____ copies of **Children's Party Book**   @ \$13.95 each   \$ _____
Please send me _____ copies of **Virginia Hospitality**   @ \$15.95 each   \$ _____
Please send me _____ copies of **Very Virginia**   @ \$17.95 each   \$ _____
Shipping and Handling   @ \$3.50 each   \$ _____
Subtotal   \$ _____
Virginia residents add 4.5% tax   \$ _____
Total   \$ _____

Name _____

Address _____

City _____ State _____ Zip _____

Make checks payable to the Junior League of Hampton Roads, Inc.

(Payable in U.S. dollars only.)

Charge to: _____ Visa _____ Mastercard   Exp. Date _____

Card Number _____

Signature _____